Pat Coombs:
The Authorised Biography

Pat Coombs

The Authorised Biography

Andrew Ross

First published in 2021 by Fantom Publishing, an imprint of Fantom Films
www.fantompublishing.co.uk

Copyright © Andrew Ross 2021

Andrew Ross has asserted his moral right to be identified as the author of this work
in accordance with the Copyright, Designs and Patents Act 1988.

A catalogue record for this book is available from the British Library.

Hardback edition ISBN: 978-1-78196-366-1

Typeset by Phil Reynolds Media Services, Leamington Spa
Printed and bound by CPI Group (UK) Ltd, Croydon, CR0 4YY

For Penny Hey

Why did I recognise you instantly?

This book would not have been possible without your help.
Thank you.

Contents

Acknowledgements

I WOULD LIKE TO THANK the following actors, agents/agencies, authors and individuals for their responses and help:

Dean Barker, Dame Floella Benjamin (Baroness Benjamin of Beckenham), Ross Devenish, Colin Edmonds, Matthew Evans, John Foster, Georgy Jamieson, Jenny Jarvis ('Frazzle Dazzle Dolls'), Richard Linford, Andrew Lynford, Scott Mitchell, Andrea Nyul, Annie Parsons, Callum J. Phoenix, Elizabeth Power, Andrew Robley, Jon Rolph, Barbara Sedassy, Paul Stephen, Bobby Warrans.

Special thanks

I am greatly indebted to the following individuals for taking the time to share with me their memories of the late Pat Coombs:

Caroline Berry, Elisabeth (Lisa) Blunt, Eleanor Bron, Gillian Bryant, Lisa Bowerman, Simon Brooks, Wilfred Brooks, Barry Burnett, Garry Bushell, Judy Buxton, Graham Cole OBE, Mike

Coleman, Sally Cryer, Dabber Davis, Steve Doherty, Jim Eldridge, Chris Emmett, Robert Gillespie, the late Eira Griffiths-Darton, Dame Sheila Hancock, Damaris Hayman, Penny Hey, Peter Hey, Jeffrey Holland, Jean Kenward (Jean Chesterman), Helen Kingman, Gary Lawson, Maurice Leonard, Tracy Lynch, Ian Masters, Paul Mayhew-Archer, Georgina Moon, Mrs Pat Morris, Jacki Piper, Georgia Ross, Michael Sharland, Sue Sinclair, John Standing, Ian Talbot OBE, Allan Taylor, Pam Valentine, Johnnie Wade, Anne Wood CBE.

I am especially grateful to Pat's niece, Penny Hey, to whom this book is dedicated. Ever since I requested to write a biography of her late aunt, Penny has been a great source of help and encouragement and without her invaluable assistance and permission to access Pat's personal archive this book would not have been possible. I would also like to thank Penny for kindly agreeing to authorise this account of her aunt's life and career.

Finally, thank you to my parents for their love and encouragement and friends for their interest in my latest book.

Preface

FROM 1997 UNTIL HER DEATH in May 2002 I was friends and pen pals with the late, much-loved actress, Pat Coombs.

As I subsequently discovered, Pat loved to write letters. I first contacted her in connection with research I was undertaking on the *Carry On* film actors and, having appeared in two films in the long-running comedy series, she duly had an entry in my first book, *Carry On Actors: The Complete Who's Who of the Carry On Film Series.*

From her very first reply Pat asked me to 'keep in touch'. I took this to be a polite, throwaway comment and I never really anticipated that we would indeed stay in regular contact. Her second letter urged me to write again if I thought she could be helpful. To my absolute delight over the course of almost five years we exchanged letters, Christmas and birthday cards, spoke on the telephone and, although I was living in Australia at the time, we managed to meet on two separate occasions.

Her letters and notes, in her clear, distinctive writing, filled with lots of exclamation marks, underlining and capital letters, were always a delight to read. Frequently written on her personalised 'compliments' slips or even on scraps of paper, Patty's letters were sincere, amusing and honest. A frugal lady, she would often send correspondence in 'recycled' envelopes and relished returning stamps which had managed to escape being postmarked.

As our friendship developed, her correspondence became more personal and heartfelt. The letters provided a unique insight into her everyday life and activities, from 'showbiz' events and her struggle with osteoporosis to her friendships and eventual move to Denville Hall, the actors' retirement home in Northwood, where she would spend the last two years of her life.

I had grown up watching Pat on television in a variety of series. I vaguely recalled her from *Ragdolly Anna*, the children's television series produced by Anne Wood (co-creator of the more famous *Teletubbies*), and also remembered seeing her funny but touching performances as 'Brown Owl' Marge Green in *EastEnders*. In the mid to late 1990s, by which time I was an adult, she was more familiar for her eccentric appearances on *Noel's House Party* as pianist Prudence (Pru) Prendergast. I had never anticipated that I would become friends with an iconic and beloved actress – my first 'famous' friend.

Through my friendship with 'Patty' I became familiar with Peggy Mount – the leading actress of stage, screen and television – with whom she had worked on television during the 1970s and early 1980s. Pat's later letters were full of titbits about her formidable and often irascible counterpart, especially after she moved into Denville Hall, where Peggy had lived since the late

1990s. As a result of Pat's anecdotes I went on to write *Everything I Ever Wanted*, a biography of Peggy's life and career, which was published in 2019. The reaction to that book and the obvious interest in Pat's life has led to this biography (a long-held personal ambition) coming to fruition.

In 1981 Pat was commissioned to write her autobiography. At the time she was very much a household name, constantly busy on television and radio and frequently seen or heard in television commercials, so it was an ideal period for her memoirs to be released. Sadly the book never got off the ground and she subsequently returned the advance to the publisher. In her conversations and letters to me at the end of her life Pat did discuss the possibility of working together to resume 'the book that never was', writing for example in April 2000 'when you come over, let's have a real get together and see if you can dig me out of my slough of despond and laziness!! Truly! If you can bear it!!'

I was honoured to be considered for the role of assisting her, but sadly time did not permit this to happen. Pat died peacefully at Denville Hall in May 2002, having battled failing health for a number of years.

Many of Pat's family members, friends and colleagues have contributed to this book and I am very grateful for their invaluable assistance. In addition to their input, as much as possible I have also allowed Pat's words to be used – via her newspaper and magazine interviews, and our own private correspondence. I hope this affectionate tribute to her life and career comes some way to fulfilling her wish of us working together on a book.

Andrew Ross, 2021

Foreword

ONE IS ASKED MANY TIMES to speak about a colleague or to try and think of a funny story about them. In this case, when asked by Andrew about Pat Coombs, no 'trying' to think of something was necessary.

Pat was the most beautiful soul, the kindest, most considerate and caring person it has been my pleasure to have known and worked with.

I had met Pat many times at charity events, some for her very own charity. Her first words were always 'How are Cherry and the children?' I remember fondly on one occasion I sat with her along with the wonderful Peggy Mount. I had the dubious pleasure of having them hold court on how much they fancied me and which one would come out the victor? It ended with a kissing contest, much to the enjoyment of those present! Peggy looked at Pat and said 'NOOOO!' as only she could, and Pat said 'I'll give him a try?' Oh! The joy for a young actor to experience these two famous and celebrated actresses using me as their foil was an experience never to be forgotten.

I worked with Pat on *Noel's House Party*, and again what a joy. To be in her presence for the camera and line run in the afternoon, being able to watch this icon work and remembering her performances and voice from my childhood, her pitch-perfect portrayal of the downtrodden, slightly nervous cardigan-wearing maiden aunt delivered with such skill – this is how I learnt my craft!

Pat was a surprise guest on my *This Is Your Life*. As I entered the studio, not knowing what was ahead for me, there was Pat sitting in the guest area on stage, blowing me a kiss, a huge smile on her face which remained there for the entire recording, a smile, a wink whenever our eyes met. Pat again spoke of Cherry and the family, and of our time spent together.

We all genuinely loved her, we miss her and like so many truly gifted artistes there will never be another. THANK YOU Pat, in my heart forever!

Graham Cole OBE, 2021

Cartoon drawings of Pat Coombs
used on two of her personalised
Christmas cards

1

Pomegranates and oranges

'I had a great childhood'

ACCORDING TO TRADITION ANY CHILD born within earshot of the bells of St Mary-le-Bow Church, Cheapside, could be defined as a 'true' Cockney. Before the hustle and bustle of modern-day traffic, the bells could apparently be heard across many parts of north and east London. A distance of just under five miles separates the Church from the birthplace of Pat Coombs, an actress who often specialised in Cockney characters during her fifty-year career on radio, film and television.

Patricia (Pat) Doreen Coombs was born at Camberwell Grove, in south-east London, on 27th August 1926. It was the year of the General Strike, which lasted for nine days, yet Pat's emergence into the world – in a leafy, well-to-do part of the nation's capital – was far removed from conflict and poor working conditions. Her birth, like much of her life, was calm, genteel and comfortable. Within six months of her arrival into the world, Pat's parents had moved a short distance to East Dulwich. Over sixty years later she would recall visiting the place where she had lived and grown up and how times had changed:

> A few years ago I went back to the house where we used to live, and sat outside in the car for ages, trying to pluck up the courage to knock on the door. As luck would have it, when I finally did, there was nobody home… but at least the house is still there, and exactly as I remember it. I think Father paid about £400 or £500 for it back in the Twenties; now it must be worth about £115,000.[1]

Just fifteen months separated the birth of Pat and her elder brother, Anthony (Tony), and in 1930 (by which time the family had moved to West Wickham in Kent) the duo became a trio with the birth of Pat's younger sister, Pamela (Pam). Pat doted on her baby sibling and would recall being sent 'round the corner' to spend the day with her maternal grandparents whilst Pam was born at home. Upon her return Pat was proudly allowed to cradle the baby on her parents' 'big bed'. Despite periods of geographical separation, the sisters would remain close for the next seven decades.

From the earliest days of her life Pat was also intensely close to her mother. Born Hilda May Ball in Nottingham in January 1898, Pat's mother was the daughter of Thomas Ball and his wife Florence (née Onion). In August 1922 she married Thomas William Coombs, ten months her junior, at Camberwell Parish Church, London, and together they had three children.[2]

Thomas Coombs was remembered by his elder daughter as a 'stern man with icy blue eyes'. A strict father, he nevertheless refused to physically chastise his daughters and Pat would admit 'he never smacked us – just a look was enough!'[3] Much of Pat's natural *joie de vivre* seems to have been inherited from her mother. The pair were often inseparable, with Pat recalling: 'Mum and I were terribly close. I was like her little shadow; wherever she went I would follow. We were very similar, like two peas in a pod... but of course I became much taller than her – and she was much prettier than me.'[4]

Penny Hey, Pat's niece, would confirm the differences in her grandparents' personalities:

> I remember Pat being extremely close to her mother; they did a lot of giggling together to my grandfather's frustration/irritation. My grandmother would gather people into her kitchen (people as in Pat and Pam's friends) and they would all sit around chatting and laughing while my grandfather would sit in the sitting room. My grandfather was a kind, honourable and moral man. Very proper but he faded into the background when my grandmother was there. She had a quick wit and naughty sense of humour. My grandfather, I think, didn't approve of Pat following her dream career but in the end he was very, very proud of her.[5]

During World War I Thomas Coombs had served in the Royal Suffolk Regiment as a 2nd Lieutenant in France. His military career was relatively short-lived after his parents 'persuaded him to resign his commission' and this was a decision his elder daughter believed he regretted for the rest of his life. Thomas's ability to resign from the army, an unusual occurrence during wartime, may well have been influenced by his father, Thomas Coombs (1870-1921), who served as Mayor of Camberwell during the Great War and who notably presided over the opening of the Camberwell YMCA 'Hut' and Gardens, which was later visited by Queen Marie of Romania.[6] Returning to civilian life to spend the next forty years working in insurance, Thomas Junior became something of a 'frustrated soldier'; so it was with pride and relish that in his early forties he joined the Home Guard (commanding his own company) as soon as World War II broke out. The experience gave him a 'terrific lift', perhaps making up in part for his brief military life twenty years earlier.

Despite the deep love between Pat and her mother, Pat was aware from an early age that her conception was probably not planned, given the slender age gap between her and Tony. Living close by were Pat's maternal grandparents, who featured heavily in her day-to-day life, and Pat would admit her grandmother was less than pleased with the sudden arrival of another grandchild. While Florence Ball, with whom Pat 'never felt particularly at ease', doted on her grandson, Tony, it was Pat's 'stone deaf' grandfather who idolised her and years later she would remember: 'We'd write little notes to one another and he used to make me laugh like nobody else I've ever known.'[7] The longevity of her maternal grandparents (they both lived into their eighties) meant they remained a key feature of Pat's life into adulthood, and her grandmother in particular was able to live long to enough to benefit from some of her granddaughter's early success as an actress, particularly on radio.

In 1969, by which time she was a well-established radio and television star, Pat would admit her one regret was that her grandfather did not 'live to be 100' so that he could have enjoyed her performance as Lucretia Tox in the BBC television production *Dombey and Son*. A great fan of the work of Charles Dickens, Grandfather Ball read a chapter from his original set of Dickens every night before bed. The books, containing original illustrations by Phiz, were later inherited by Pat (who subsequently bequeathed them to her niece, Sally Cryer).

Pat readily admitted throughout her life that she was not from a theatrical family, calling them 'very conventional'; but her maternal grandfather did write and revise some plays and always wanted to go into the theatre, while her mother, who was clearly a vivacious personality in her own right, was always very supportive of Pat's future career choice. It was via the Ball side of the family that Pat appears to have inherited her artistic talent for voices, acting and writing.

Unlike many of her future friends and colleagues, Pat enjoyed a blissful infancy. 'I had a great childhood,' she would recall; and, despite the impact of the General Strike and the horrors of the Great Depression, the Coombs family enjoyed a relatively comfortable lifestyle with Thomas Coombs managing to remain in secure employment throughout his working life. In later years Pat would recall being given pocket money once a week and saving up for a 'splurge' at the sweet shop: 'Milky Way was 1d., a Mars bar was 2d., and I can remember having a passion for Eucalyptus Gums at 2d. a quarter. You see, we weren't allowed many sweet things in those days – a chocolate biscuit was a treat.' A further treat in the Coombs household was 'pomegranate night' on a Friday as Pat would remember: 'Ooh, the excitement! That or an orange with a lump of sugar on it. Looking back, it doesn't sound very exciting does it? Pomegranates are full of pips, and oranges aren't exactly exotic – but, believe me, when Mum put them on the table we were the happiest kids in Christendom.'[8]

During Pat's early childhood the family owned a car, a relative rarity in the 1930s, and in their little black and red

Morris Eight they would journey to seaside resorts including Bournemouth and Worthing where Pat's love of entertaining really began. While admitting that she was never a 'show-off' as a child, Pat quickly realised that she had a talent for mimicking others, particularly her sister Pam and their cousins. This talent displayed itself from about 1932 onwards but in 1936, when Pat took part in an Empire Day tableau, she would remember 'shaking like a leaf' because she was so nervous. Ironically, she would often be cast as timid, mousy characters during her long career, particularly in her roles on television.

The Coombs family spent many happy hours at the seaside and throughout her life Pat enjoyed being by the coast. It was during an early family holiday in Worthing where she saw a concert party that Pat became hooked on the joys of entertainment, and in later life she would often recall 'falling in love with a gypsy violinist and everyone else in the show'.[9] By the age of six Pat already knew she wanted to be an actress.

Despite her early love of entertaining Pat grew up to be something of a 'tomboy' and this was one factor which saw the early close relationship she had had with her brother quickly disappear. According to Pat 'he wasn't in the least bit interested in either of his sisters. Openly and often he would complain that he wanted to be the only one. Perhaps it was a great big front he put on… I don't know. But it used to sadden me because I desperately wanted to be friends. It was alright when we were little, but from the time I was six I wasn't allowed to join in his games… and I really wanted to be part of his gang.'[10]

After initially being round-faced and somewhat cherub-like, Pat developed into a slightly quirky-looking child. Her time as a pupil at Beckenham's County School for Girls was not always an easy one and she frequently admitted to hating her time there.[11] Her height and 'beanpole' figure made her a prime target for bullies; yet she made it her mission to disarm her assailants with comedy, later saying: 'I think it is quite pleasant if people can laugh at you and with you. It is a great joy making people laugh and it is so near the other thing anyway. The difference between comedy and tragedy is very slight.'[12] In this respect Pat was not dissimilar to another great comedy actress, the *Carry On* star Hattie Jacques. Having always been 'larger than life' (with her weight by the age of fifty reaching twenty stone), Hattie would famously say 'when you're my size, you become conditioned to people making jokes about you. You have to make them laugh with you rather than at you.' Although she knew from an early age that she wanted to perform, Pat would later admit 'I was too scared to tell the teachers at school I wanted to be an actress, in case they all laughed at me,' and as a result she received no formal training as an actress during her formative years.[13]

By the age of eighteen, while World War II still raged, Pat had been out of school for a couple of years and was working as a kindergarten teacher. It was classified as a reserved occupation and as a result she did not see active service, unlike her brother who went on to join the Royal Navy. Despite being gainfully employed, Pat's ambitions to be an actress never left her, and having known from such an early age where her ambitions lay she never gave up on her dream. Her friendship with the future actress Vivien Merchant proved to be a life-changing one and she was easily swayed by Vivien to go to drama lessons, as she would later recall:

7

> Ada Thompson, as Vivien was then, was about 13 and used to visit the people next door in West Wickham, Kent, where we were living. We chatted over the garden fence and she persuaded me to have some private drama lessons with her tutor. We used to go to lessons together, during the flying bombs.[14]

The decision had the full backing of at least one of Pat's parents and she would admit, 'My mother had been all for the idea.'[15]

Three years younger than Pat, Ada Thompson (under the stage name Vivien Merchant) went on to become a BAFTA-winning actress, also receiving a Tony award nomination in 1967 for her role in Harold Pinter's *The Homecoming*. She had married playwright Harold Pinter in 1956 and two years later had a son, Daniel. For a time the couple were friends with Pat and photographs of the young family would feature in her scrapbooks. Although Vivien would appear in many of Harold's plays, their marriage sadly collapsed in the mid 1960s (they eventually divorced in 1980) and she would die from alcoholism in October 1982 at the age of fifty-three.

However, despite her own tragic end, it was thanks to Ada's assistance that Pat went on to enrol at LAMDA (the London Academy of Music and Dramatic Art) having gained a 'Victory Scholarship' immediately after the end of the Second World War. Pat made many friends during her time at drama school and amongst her fellow students were a host of future stars including LAMDA's youngest ever pupil, Diana Dors (labelled 'Diano' Dors in Pat's scrapbooks).

Also there at the time was Irene ('Rene') Sutcliffe who would be a constant figure in Pat's life over the next fifty years. Born Ethel Irene Sutcliffe in Burnley, the daughter of an ironmonger,

Irene was two years older than Pat. Like her LAMDA chum, she rose to fame in the 1950s before securing a place in television history in 1968 when she joined the cast of *Coronation Street* as shopkeeper Maggie Clegg.[16] While still studying at LAMDA the two friends formed a club, named 'The Octopus', which took its name from the play *Dear Octopus*. In 1950 Irene, by then a member of the well-known Harry Hanson repertory company, married fellow actor George Cooper (not to be confused with actor George A. Cooper) and over the years, like Pat, progressed into all areas of the profession.

One of Pat's greatest influences at drama school was Frieda Hodgson who was considered 'one of the most highly regarded drama teachers of the post-war era'. Eccentric-looking and invariably dressed in long black frocks with frilled necks and cuffs, Hodgson was the embodiment of 'commitment and constructive criticism' and continued to work in the profession until the very end of her long life (she died in 1992).[17] Among her many tutees, apart from Pat, were the likes of Richard Harris, Janet Suzman and David Suchet.

After about eighteen months at the Academy, by which time she had graduated, Pat began teaching accents, revealing later: 'They found me so difficult to launch, as I knew they would. I seem to hang on there forever. After my first year I taught dialects.'[18] Pat's flair for 'voices' was a natural gift. It was used professionally of course, and also privately as a defence mechanism throughout her life to disguise her shyness. In real life Pat would frequently slip into 'funny' voices or accents, ranging from broad Cockney to 'mock refined'. There was never a time when she was unable to transform her voice, and in her forties she would reveal:

> I don't know why, but I have always been able to pick up dialects –
> or even an individual's way of speaking – very quickly. I probably
> started by imitating our Scots neighbours in West Wickham... and
> earlier my baby sister and cousin crying.[19]

By the time she reached maturity Pat was very tall for her generation of women, standing just over five feet eight inches in height. Throughout her career the taunts she had endured at school continued and she was frequently described in the press as 'lanky' or 'beanpole'. Neither of the adjectives was flattering. Her childhood resilience continued into adulthood and being self-effacing remained Pat's greatest strength. She herself was under no illusions about her looks, saying, 'I am terribly thin and the nose is a bit huge for the face,' and she admitted she had the 'pipe-cleaner look'.[20] When likened to the 'spaghetti-like' cartoon character Olive Oyl (of *Popeye* fame) she would concede: 'Well, it's true isn't it? I do look like Olive Oyl. Of course, I can see it.'[21] Much later in her career she was more accepting of her appearance and realised its advantages, saying: 'To be honest I would have liked to have experienced the glamour bit. When I started out I thought, "Well, I'm far too tall and far too plain, so who's going to employ me?" But they have and it's been wonderful.'[22]

From her earliest days at LAMDA Pat was profoundly aware that she was not cut out to be a serious dramatic actress. When cast in straight roles at drama school, she would divulge, her classmates 'soon started to fall about, willy-nilly'.[23] Although she would go on to play a handful of dramatic parts on television – notably as Miss Tox in *Dombey and Son* and Miss Pole, the village gossip, in *Cranford* – it was undoubtedly as a comedy actress that Pat would make her name.[24] Without the looks of a leading lady Pat felt that her strongest chances of success within the acting profession lay in radio: 'heard and not seen, I thought,' she admitted in 1972.[25] From the very beginning of her career Pat was indeed adamant that she wanted to be a radio actress, and at the end of her life would say: 'Radio's all I ever wanted to do. I never wanted to be seen, ever. I looked at myself in the mirror at the age of seven, stuck my tongue out and thought, you're a plain, ugly little madam. And I thought, voices yes, faces no. Who would want to see it? I didn't want to go on television, but it happened anyway.'[26]

In real life Pat was naturally funny and as a result genuinely enjoyed comic roles. Unlike many actresses of her era she never particularly felt pigeonholed or typecast, and after thirty years in the profession would say:

> With me the comedy bit was always there. I never wanted to play St Joan or any of those serious parts. I was never a leading lady. The only talent I ever had was for mimicry and doing funny voices. There I was, very tall, very thin, with this face. It's a funny face, which does make up rather easily into all these funny old ladies I seem to play so often.[27]

After finally leaving LAMDA, Pat's first professional job was in repertory theatre in Scunthorpe. By 1948 she was listed in the famous *Spotlight* casting directory under 'juvenile-character women'. Boasting skills as an 'expert' in all accents and dialects, Pat was now trying her best to establish herself as a jobbing actress. Further work in rep would follow, and so began the long years of building up her craft the hard way. Although this allowed her to gain both professional experience and confidence the theatre held no real attraction for Pat. Her early stage work involved the rigours of weekly rep with twice nightly performances, being 'ASM' (Assistant Stage Manager) and doing 'small parts'. While she enjoyed acting in a variety of roles the technical side of theatre life did not appeal to Pat, primarily, by her own admission, because she 'wasn't very good at it'. One of her main duties in one theatre was to paint flowers onto white china teacups every week to alternate the pattern. This inevitably led to Pat running out of time to complete the job and only painting one half of the cups! She was even sacked from one production after failing to ensure a door on set had the required key to open it. The door (unusually boasting a real lock and key) ended up being locked and Pat would recall with genuine hilarity that this meant the leading lady had to enter the stage via the fireplace, rather than the door itself. After such disasters during her fifty-year career Pat rarely took to the stage. She was happy to 'disappear' from the world of theatre, but never regretted her decision to concentrate on work on radio and television.

Despite her flair for mimicry, her initial auditions on radio for *Much-Binding-in-the-Marsh* and *ITMA* (*It's That Man Again*) were not successful, and for the latter series she lost out to Hattie Jacques. However, Pat did make a significant impression with the BBC's powers that be and they promised to 'keep in touch'. They were true to their word. In 1947 she made her radio debut in *The Rowse Murder*, one of a series of Scotland Yard cases starring Clive Brook for Radio Luxembourg. New-Zealand-born radio scriptwriter Ted Kavanagh (the man behind *ITMA*) was so impressed with her skills that he subsequently invited her to join his group, as Pat would remember:

> He infiltrated me on the air, through programmes like the Michael Howard and Derek Roy shows and finally in *The Arthur Askey Show*.[28]

Gradually offers of work began to come Pat's way. In the BBC radio play *The Atomic Duck* (the story of a duck which causes a sensation by laying an egg of pure uranium) she effectively did the work of six actresses by providing six different voices. Another turning point was marked when she played a two-line part in the original *A Life of Bliss* radio series but stayed on with the production, playing everything from crying babies to dumb maids. In 1952 Pat was hired on the spot by BBC producer-playwright Ian Messiter after she read to him over the telephone a paragraph from a newspaper in a variety of dialects. Her years of mimicry had seemingly paid off.

In the very early days of starting out in the business Pat had also wanted to develop her skills as a singer and consequently took lessons in an attempt to improve her voice and range. During the course of her coaching she suffered a severe accident, which unfortunately put her career on hold for almost two years, as she would later reveal:

> I must have overdone some breathing exercises. I felt a terrible pain and realised something had gone wrong. A specialist told me part of my left lung had collapsed. [29]

Pat was admitted to hospital for a month, and for years after suffered from what she later called 'a popping lung'. As part of her convalescence (under doctor's orders) she was prescribed work in the open air and went to work at a garden nursery in Bromley, Kent, where she would also return when she could not secure work as an actress. Decades later during her *This Is Your Life* tribute, the owners of the nursery, Jeffrey and Hazel Hester, would remember Pat's nimble fingers and natural gift for voices and accents.

Although she had been given a taste of success on radio, the early years of Pat's career were far from easy. She would later recall:

> I had many periods out of work. Once I went a whole year without getting a part. I drew the dole and there were even times when I reached the dole limit and made do without! On occasions I fell back on jobs outside acting. I went back to the kindergarten, where I taught for three years altogether, I taught acting, I babysat.[30]

In 1949, the year in which she appeared on radio in *Here's Howard* (with Michael Howard), she would write that things remained 'unbelievably discouraging'. While refusing to give up entirely on her dream of being an actress she did begin to wonder whether it was 'the worst job I ever got mixed up in!'

While still living with her parents and when not working she occupied her time with everyday tasks. She revelled in normality and continued to do so throughout her life. In 1969 she would say 'there's always plenty to do in the house and garden, and I try to get on with it and pretend there is no such thing as the telephone. But it's only existing really and when finally the phone rings and there is a job for me I come to life again.'[31] She remained a home bird, and over the years various changes of address came as Pat's parents moved fairly frequently: from 7 The Drive, West Wickham, Kent, to 118 Copse Avenue in West Wickham, to 2 The Welkins, Hickman Lane in Lindfield and later to the coastal village of Saltdean. On each occasion Pat duly accompanied her parents while also later maintaining a small bedsit flat in Swiss Cottage, London, which proved useful when she was working in the city.

2

Speak as you find, that's my motto

'Nola was such a stupid woman'

LONG BEFORE TELEVISION SETS BECAME an essential fixture in homes across the country, radio had established itself as a trusted provider of family entertainment. During the dark days of the Second World War the wireless was not only essential for communication but also provided much-needed relief for young and old alike.

The medium helped make careers for numerous writers, producers and directors and made stars of many actors who would later become household names. Within the space of a few short years, series such as *ITMA* (*It's That Man Again*) and *Ray's A Laugh* (starring Ted Ray) had become extremely popular. By the 1950s there were three main BBC radio stations broadcasting in Britain, and a host of programmes, including *The Goon Show, The Clitheroe Kid, Beyond Our Ken* and *Hancock's Half Hour*, had become firm favourites. Several would even continue to attract audiences well into the 1960s.

Hello Playmates, a radio series written by Bob Monkhouse and Denis Goodwin, propelled Pat to fame and throughout her career she was fondly remembered as Nola, the 'taciturn, unwilling, unmarriageable' daughter of office cleaner Mrs Purvis, played by the delightful and much-loved Irene Handl. The role brought Pat instant recognition within the industry and to the public at large and in many ways secured her place as a radio star – a title she would hold until the very end of her life.

Pat had known Bob Monkhouse for years. The pair lived in the same area and she was a guest at his twenty-first birthday celebrations in June 1949. She became good friends with Bob and his first wife, Elizabeth Thompson, and would often babysit their young children.[1] Pat adored working with Bob and Denis Goodwin, once saying: 'What I appreciate more than anything – and I'm speaking as a performer now – is their lovely, calm attitude to everything. No panic, no fuss: just a pleasant reassuring belief that however hectic life becomes, it'll be alright.'[2] By 1952 Pat was professionally represented by the Bob Monkhouse and Denis Goodman Agency; as Monkhouse would later jokingly recall, she was 'their only client!' Six years later Pat would discuss her association with the pair:

> I'd been in repertory and I'd been given masses of BBC auditions – schools and drama, just a Wednesday matinee now and again, no comedy to speak of at all. Somehow it came out that I 'did' voices and the boys paid me the great compliment of seeming to have faith in me. When they were writing *Hip, Hip Hoo-Roy* for Derek Roy, I found myself in the show and speaking their lines for the first time. I like to believe that they think of me rather as a lucky mascot. They put me in a show even if I have only one line to say![3]

Also at the centre of the agency was Dabber Davis who at the age of ninety-three would recall 'discovering' Bob Monkhouse after the war:

> When we started originally it was Dabber Davis Productions. I had the licence because in those days the Lord Chamberlain insisted agents must have a licence… I discovered Bob Monkhouse… he was in the RAF, and I'd come out of the army about three or four years before and in the war, and indeed after the war a little bit, they used to have American stage door canteens and it was for army, navy, air force, and if you were in uniform you could do a 'turn'. By that time I was an agent and was looking for new talent. This was 1949. I started as a comic and I saw Bob at the Nuffield Centre – a callow youth, but very funny and he had the gift of comedy, of timing and beautiful delivery and he was very good for a young bloke.

Dabber remains in awe of what he describes as Bob Monkhouse's 'marvellous talent' and admits they became 'like brothers'. Although Monkhouse was not immune to criticism, with Dabber recalling that 'some unpleasant critics called him the oily boy because of his American style', he became one of the country's biggest stars in the 1950s and would remain so until his death in 2003.

Dabber's insight into the professional relationship between Bob Monkhouse and Denis Goodwin is unparalleled and he likens them in many ways to Jewel and Warriss (Jimmy Jewel and Ben Warriss, the famous comedy act who worked together for more than thirty years). Sadly, as Dabber recollects, the partnership was not an equal one and although Denis was a 'brilliant scriptwriter' he was a 'terrible performer'. Eventually Bob and Denis went their separate ways with Denis moving to America for a time to work for Bob Hope's writing team. The early success Denis had enjoyed seemed to evaporate upon his return to Britain and Dabber Davis admits: 'Denis drank himself to death – working with him was impossible because he was so pissed all the time.'[4]

Hello Playmates was hailed as 'The Most Promising New Programme of the Year'. The star of the show was Arthur Askey (who had begun his radio career in the 1930s) and he was paired with the magician and television personality David Nixon. The *Radio Times* would describe the duo as a 'perfect team':

> David is six foot two, gentle and unassuming; Arthur is five foot four, brash and ebullient. They attracted each other like the north and south poles of a magnet... Each is funny in his own particular style and each is sparked off the other as flint on steel.[5]

Handl and Coombs were hailed as stars in their own right. Born in London in 1901, the daughter of an Austrian banker, Irene Handl had been a late starter to the acting profession having made her name on stage as the Cockney Maid in the London production of *George and Margaret* in 1937. She went on to become a beloved actress on stage, screen, television and radio and also wrote three novels. Handl's role as the 'glorious, shouting malaprop' Mrs Purvis ('the studio cleansing executive') was declared by critics as 'the funniest discovery in the new Askey show'.[6] Her catchphrase of 'Nola, babsie' quickly caught on, as did the frequent reply – 'Yes, Mum' – of her daughter. Irene would reveal 'I take my false teeth out to get the accent better', and she also insisted that she and Pat dressed up as their respective characters.[7] Over forty years later Pat would remember 'but we *did* perform in front of an audience and it made it feel so real somehow!'[8]

Pat adored Irene and would later say: 'I can say how terrific the many, many times I worked with Irene Handl [were]... she was an absolute joy and became a No. 1 friend… I will never forget our radio series with Arthur Askey.'[9] Over the years the two ladies were frequently reunited, on stage, television and radio, and remained firm friends. Dabber Davis remembers Pat and Irene with affection:

> Pat was a lovely lady and a very good, talented actress. We used to have them [Pat and Irene] in all the shows… Pat with her dolly poe hat and dress from the 1920s and Irene saying 'all for you sir'… Many artists found them impossible to work with because they were just so hilarious. Cyril Fletcher went hysterical – he couldn't work – he said it was the funniest thing he'd ever seen.

Likewise Dabber would reveal that singer Sheila Buxton (who appeared on *Starstruck*, hosted by Bob Monkhouse and Denis Goodwin) was also unable to perform because she was giggling so much having seen Pat and Irene dressed as their respective characters. Husband-and-wife thespians Michael Denison and Dulcie Gray, well known for their numerous appearances on stage, screen and television, meanwhile 'collapsed with laughter on the floor' upon seeing Mrs Purvis and Nola.[10]

The strength of the character of Nola proved to be a double-edged sword for Pat. In some ways the persona of the cleaner's none-too-bright daughter would never really leave her, and long after the series had ended Nola's oft-heard catchphrase 'Speak as you find, that's my motto!' remained instantly recognisable. In 1972 Pat would say: 'Nola was such a stupid woman. A complete nit, but I loved her dearly. I'm afraid that I became typed for quite a while through playing her.'[11]

In 1954/55, while Irene Handl was busy touring in a stage production of Noël Coward's *Blithe Spirit*, Pat was cast to appear in *Fast and Loose*, another series by Bob Monkhouse and

Denis Goodwin. Once again she revelled in the opportunity to work with the successful writers, albeit without her lovably eccentric sidekick.

In the summer of 1956 Pat was again back on stage, working with actor and comedian Dick Emery for the first time in *Dazzle* at the Sparrow's Nest Theatre in Lowestoft. This was the start of a professional partnership and cherished friendship which would last until Dick's death in 1983. The production was well received, with one critic writing: 'Dick Emery brings his own brand of crazy comedy to the show... plus a rather pleasant singing voice,' while Pat also received praise for having a 'change of voice and face to fit all the varying moods and situations of the comedy sketches'.[12] Thankfully Pat was now gaining work in all areas of the business including appearing alongside Max Bygraves in Val Parnell's *Spectacular* series in 1956 (together with Peter Sellers, Vi Stevens and a very young Bernard Bresslaw). Increasingly she was becoming well known thanks to her work on the 'wireless', and her skill and professionalism would ensure she worked with some of the country's top comedy actors throughout the remainder of the 1950s.

Terry Scott and Bill Maynard became two of Britain's most successful television stars in the 1970s with respective credits including *Terry and June* and *Oh No It's Selwyn Froggitt*. Over a decade earlier the pair enjoyed success together on the small screen in three series of *Great Scott – It's Maynard!*, a sketch show which allowed them to showcase their comic talents. Having made his stage debut supporting Terry Scott in 1951, Bill Maynard was happy to star opposite Scott whose own career began after he was demobbed from the Royal Navy. With leading lady Shirley Eaton and popular comedy actor

Hugh Lloyd also appearing in the first series of the show, Pat (who had encountered Terry Scott years earlier during the recording of *Here's Howard*) joined the established team for series two and three, both of which aired in 1956. Having completed six episodes of the series it was reported in the press that the cast went their separate ways for the summer of 1956, with Bill Maynard working in summer shows at Weymouth, Terry Scott and Hugh Lloyd going to Felixstowe and Pat joining Dick Emery in Torquay.

By now Pat had been a working actress for almost a decade, and although television was still in its relative infancy she was already beginning to make her mark on the small screen. Her success on the radio led to two guest appearances on the popular television series *Hancock's Half Hour* (playing Matilda in 'The Great Detective' in 1957 and a Saxon Princess in 'Ericson the Viking' the following year), and so reliable and versatile was she as a performer that many other leading comedy actors of the day requested her. A personal favourite among Pat's many leading men was Ted Ray, and while being interviewed during one of her many appearances with him she would say of her growing reputation, 'Please call me a lady comic and leave it at that.' In similar vein to her character of Nola, Pat was cast to play 'that terrible character', the daily help, in *Ray's A Laugh* – a long-running radio series which had begun in 1949. Pat would reveal at the time: 'It's not really hard work. Only half a day a week, but the money is good and enough to live on.'

Live performances on television and radio helped build Pat's confidence as an actress, but there was no room for error. In 1989 she would recall the salad days of her career:

It was wonderful but a bit frightening too. Everything was live so it was doubly nerve-racking. But the business had such heart then. There was a real togetherness which is not as noticeable today. But that could just be nostalgia on my part.[13]

By 1958, when she played Miss Ursula Prune in another series of *Ray's A Laugh*, Pat was regarded as 'one of those exclusive band of women laughtermakers... in a class of her own'; and in the following year she was appearing in *The Cyril Fletcher Show*, a comedy sketch series given to Cyril by ITV impresario Jack Hylton, which also featured Cyril's wife, Betty Astell.[14]

As well as revelling in her time spent with Ted Ray and Cyril Fletcher (who in the 1950s were two of Britain's top comedy stars), another comedian Pat considered key in her career was Charlie Drake – the pint-sized actor, singer and writer, well known for his catchphrase 'Hello, my darlings'. Drake was not always the easiest of performers to work with and actress Judy Cornwell, who appeared alongside Pat and Henry McGee in *The Charlie Drake Show* in 1961, would recall him as 'a strange man', revealing in her autobiography how Pat knew just how to handle her colleague's eccentric behaviour:

Charlie Drake introduced himself but behaved quite differently from anyone I had ever worked with before. He was more an observer than a participant. He was watching us all as we read. Someone else, his small stand-in, was reading his part. At the end of the read-through Charlie Drake went into a huddle with Shaun O'Riordan, the director, and one actor was called over. After a minute's discussion the actor left the rehearsal room never to return.

'What's that all about?' I asked Pat Coombs.

'Don't ask, don't look, you didn't see anything,' she replied with an overbright smile, as if we were discussing anything but the show.[15]

Although now well established as an actress on radio and television, Pat avoided the world of celebrity and maintained a quiet private life. At the age of thirty she was still living at home with her parents and sister, admitting at the time, 'We have a lot of fun together. In fact it's a bit of a madhouse. When it gets too crazy I can always go and stay at my flat in London. That is if I'm earning enough money.'[16] While her reputation as an actress was growing, Pat's feet remained firmly on the ground. She would watch from the sidelines over the next few years as many actresses of her generation disappeared from the profession. Many had been light leading ladies, groomed by the Rank 'Charm School' to appear in films of the 1950s. Largely regarded as 'decoration' in many of their appearances, the careers of such actresses inevitably petered out as their looks began to fade. Others simply chose to leave the profession to concentrate on marriage and family life. Pat meanwhile continued to work hard to fulfil her childhood dream, never aiming to get her name in lights above the title of a production but simply wanting to work and entertain.

3
Moo and Moolie

'The one I should have married'

ON THURSDAY 13TH DECEMBER 1951 it was announced in the local press that Pat had become engaged to Radio Officer John Mark Sutton, the only son of Mr and Mrs F. A. J. Sutton of Goodhart Way, West Wickham.[1] John was a friend of Pat's brother, Tony, and was one of a number of young bachelors she had met via her older sibling.

The union proved to be short-lived. Twenty years after the engagement was called off, Pat would remember that John's lack of confidence regarding his height (he was an inch or two shorter than her) was one of the reasons the relationship broke down – along with her own 'cold feet' and desire to pursue a career as an actress.[2] In 1976 she would recall:

> We were poles apart. He was as wild as I'm not. He was a bit like the sailor with a girl in every port. That's all right. What I didn't see, the

heart didn't grieve over. But he worried because I was in show business. He couldn't believe I would be faithful when he was at sea. I would have been. I can't think why he didn't trust me, 'specially when he was playing around.[3]

As Pat remembered, when the relationship ended John 'went off to sail around the world but instead he met a girl in Scotland and was married within seven weeks'.[4] Ironically, although it was seen at the time to be a 'rebound' union, he settled into being a 'model husband and father'.[5]

Happily the break-up between Pat and John was amicable and in her sixties she would reveal how she had kept her engagement ring:

The day I returned it his mum opened the door. I said 'Give this to John' and she said 'No, if you don't want to remember him, then keep it and remember me.' I couldn't wear it for years, but now I wouldn't be without it, because I've since met up with John and we're great friends again. He's a grandad now.[6]

Years later, when Pat again discussed the romance in an interview, John's children were in their twenties and she had met his wife who, when she saw the aforementioned engagement ring, jokingly said 'That's more than I ever had!'[7]

John's career in the Navy at least allowed Pat to inject her own unique brand of humour into the story of her short-lived engagement, and whenever she talked about her relationship with a sailor she was keen to point out that her love life was 'all at sea'.[8]

A more lasting romance came via her friendship with actor George Raistrick. Born in Lincolnshire in March 1931, George was almost five years Pat's junior and would go on to become a prolific jobbing actor in theatre, film and television. It was many years after her engagement ended that Pat became romantically involved with George, although by that stage they had been friends for more than a decade and he was a regular visitor to the Coombs household. Private correspondence from 1962 reveals that the pair saw so much of each during the previous year that they had decided to marry. However, the discussed nuptials never came to fruition, a decision Pat labelled 'sad, but sensible'.

Despite not marrying, Pat and George remained good friends for the next thirty years. He was frequently referred to by Pat as 'the one I *should* have married' although she rarely mentioned George by his full name. In a 1989 interview, discussing her 1951 engagement and later relationship with George, she would say: 'I'm even closer with my other old flame. He was an actor and he's the one I really should have married. I got cold feet. We're still in touch and we still regret not walking down the aisle'.[9] Pat certainly never forgot George, and writer Pam Valentine, who became good friends with Pat in the late 1970s, would remember Pat describing him as 'the love of my life'.[10]

It would appear that despite their close relationship Pat and George's union remained purely platonic. When asked in later life if she had any other regrets she would reply: 'Well, I'm a bit prudish, slightly old-fashioned: I still believe in the old values... but I shouldn't regret that, should I?'[11]

The comment would appear to be a fair indication that Pat remained a virgin. Sex before marriage would have been frowned upon by a lady, like Pat, who had firm morals. Such morals had been instilled in her from birth and she never deviated from them. Despite the often open-minded profession in which she worked, Pat herself was steadfast in her views. She did not, for example, believe in unmarried couples living together, even as times and principles changed in the 1970s and beyond. Although she kept her thoughts and judgements on such matters largely to herself, those who knew her well were abundantly aware of her opinion. Pat was 'old-fashioned' – and she stayed that way.

A decade after her relationship with George ended, Pat revealed that her own 'stupidity' was the cause behind the pair parting ways. On the subject of marriage and children she would say:

> Yes, yes, yes, yes, I do feel a general regret at not having children. I started out with the idea of having four and that dwindled to one as I got older. No, I haven't really dismissed the idea of marriage. Do women ever dismiss the idea? I don't think so. It might happen. You never know. But you do get terribly used to being alone. You get very selfish. [12]

Two handwritten postcards from George were preserved in Pat's personal archive. Written circa 1989, they are a record of their fifty-year friendship and give a brief but unique insight into a relationship which endured over the decades. They are recorded, in part, below:

> Dearest Mool,
>
> My proposed trip to town has so far not materialised – apart that is from a visit to the 'courts', not for any misdemeanour of mine but to gain a little background for my forthcoming TV appearance as a prosecuting counsel. Fascinating! Much better than anything Jeffrey Archer can come up with – which was not a lot according to that prostitute. However *Baker's Wife* is happening – going to the Phoenix would you believe! So will be in from late August for rehearsals – then a merry meet! Hope EE [*EastEnders*] is going well and the schedule is not too demanding... Lots of love Moolie

As a postscript George would write:

> 'Up the Brownies' or would that be thought of as some form of deviant behaviour? [13]

The second card reads:

> Hello Mool,
>
> Sorry couldn't make 'town' this week, too much to do after the workmen have been in. You know what they are like! Hopefully I'll be up next week. I must contact Rene [Irene Sutcliffe] to find out about Frieda's do but have doubts about making it. We could all get together and send some flowers! Still haven't seen you on the omnibus, had to go out last Sunday and didn't get back in time. Will try again this weekend. Hope you're OK and not trumping too violently with all the pressure. Much love Moolie. [14]

George was an interesting character in his own right and it is easy to see why Pat remained so very fond of him. Having left school at the age of fourteen, he moved from his home in Grimsby to study at LAMDA where he first met Pat. George went on to tour the country in rep with the Harry Hanson company before being called up for National Service in 1949, spending time in the Royal Air Force. During his years away from acting he pursued a career as a gentlemen's outfitter in the bespoke tailoring department of Austin Reed before his return to LAMDA in 1964.

Lisa Blunt, George's partner during the last fifteen years of his life, explained his early career and belated dramatic training:

> I think he had a riot in London! After a year, the lure of work and wages meant he left and joined a touring actors' group. By now it would be the early 50s. There was a period when George married and left the stage. Neither worked out. He returned to LAMDA, was awarded a gold medal and returned to the stage.

On a more private level Lisa would further recall:

> I have many memories of George – personal and professional. He
> was a much loved member of theatrical companies – loyal, reliable,
> fun, professional and not prone to meltdowns! I remember him with
> his dark chocolate timbre of voice, wearing his fedora through the
> winter and with time to devote to each person he met, making them
> feel that being with them was all that he was interested in.[15]

Upon his return to the profession George Raistrick continued to work prodigiously as an actor in all areas of the
medium, without ever becoming a household name. During
the 1980s he was kept extremely busy working on stage for the
Royal Shakespeare Company in a variety of productions, and
between 1973 and 1995 alone appeared in well over a hundred
plays. In the 1990s, as well as continuing his stage work, he
made many guest appearances on television in a number of
popular series including *Inspector Morse*, *Minder*, *Common as
Muck* (four episodes), *Pie in the Sky* and *The Thin Blue Line*.
He was still working on television until his death (with several
appearances being screened posthumously), and was also performing on stage in *La Grande Magia* at the Lyttelton Theatre
in London just hours before he passed away. He had earlier
received rave reviews for his appearance as Colonel Pickering
in *Pygmalion* at the beginning of 1995, in what was considered
a 'definitive performance of the part'.[16]

News that George had collapsed and died at his home in
the early hours of 12th September 1995 at the age of sixty-four
came as a tremendous shock to family, friends and colleagues.
The National Theatre's artistic director Richard Eyre, who had
directed George in his final performance, would later say: 'He
was someone who was universally loved – and that's not just

a pious sentiment. George was a first-rate character actor, a very droll man, warm-hearted, skilful and extremely good company.'[17]

The sudden death of George Raistrick must have stirred many emotions for Pat. Over the years the pair had remained in contact and stayed friends. Like Pat, he was good at keeping in touch via telephone calls, cards and letters and enjoyed writing 'the occasional doggerel', a collection of which was made by Lisa after his death, entitled *Raistrick's Ramblings*.

Interestingly, Pat was a beneficiary in George's will, dated 2nd February 1989 (he left a net estate valued at £157, 329).[18] In addition to leaving provision for his elderly mother (in the event that she outlived him) and bequests to others including his brother and sister-in-law, George left the sum of £250 to Pat. Although her thoughts on this are unknown, she would surely have been touched and grateful to be remembered by her dear friend.

*

In her mid forties Pat was still open to the possibility of getting married but realised she had left it too late to start a family, saying in 1972: 'I would like to get married. I'm not one of those completely independent people. The only pity is that now it would be too late for children.'[19]

Pat very sensibly realised that her success as an actress would have enabled her to give a child a privileged upbringing. At the height of her professional success she admitted:

> I'm very nicely off and it would have been a bit of treatsville for them – extra pennies from mum towards education and things like that.

Fortunately, I have nephews and nieces and can do things in a small way for them.[20]

The full extent of how much Pat longed for a husband and children will forever remain a mystery, although she frequently claimed 'I would have loved to have children'[21] and it was almost heartbreaking when she said 'I regret it in many ways. There won't be any children now. But at least I can't ever upset anyone but myself. I can't ruin another person's life.'[22]

The example of her own parents' long marriage enabled Pat to see how a really good relationship could withstand the passage of time. It was, in many ways, a tough act to follow. Both her siblings had failed marriages (and in the case of her brother Tony, two failed marriages) and this must have preyed on her mind when she met potential suitors. In 1976 she would say:

I always fall for the wrong ones. It's my fault I haven't married. People sometimes say I was looking for perfection, but of course you never find it.[23]

Pat had an idealised image of her perfect 'Mister' – the man she wanted to meet and settle down with, but never did:

It really was slippers by the fire, but the chemistry doesn't work that way. My pleasures are terribly simple. I'm a stop-at-home. I enjoy people in small doses. I take a lot of getting to a party. There is this image of 'Pat's fun' which is nice and I hope I am. But I can still walk into a crowded room and think 'Oh, my Gawd, I wish I hadn't come.' I'd rather be home reading a book or watching telly.'[24]

She was also painfully aware of the pressures placed upon marriages by the constraints of show business and fame, saying in 1977:

> I'm old fashioned enough to believe that if I enter into that sort of
> contract, well that's IT. But over the years I've been disillusioned. I
> thought marriage was lovely but then I've looked around and seen
> the misery of some marriages. It's super if you do have a solid
> marriage in show business and, of course, there are some – but I
> rather think they're the exceptions, don't you? [25]

Despite her lifelong lack of confidence regarding her looks
– her height, 'beanpole' figure and prominent nose – Pat was
attractive to the opposite sex. She was funny, intelligent and
entertaining. Her slim figure never left her and even in her
forties she still only weighed eight and a half stone, admitting
'I've only put on 4lb in ten years.'[26] Many felt it was a shame
Pat never married or had a family of her own. Actress Sue
Sinclair, who became friends with Pat in her final years, confirmed this sentiment:

> I seem to remember my mother telling me that Pat had parted from
> the love of her life some years before and it was someone she should
> have married (he may have been married already?); it seemed des-
> perately sad in the life of someone who had given others such joy.[27]

Within the acting profession Pat caught the attention of a
number of colleagues and contemporaries. She was especially
close to Dick Emery, with whom she frequently performed
over a period of three decades. Dick married five times and as
a result was described by actor Harry Fowler as 'a bachelor
who got married – now and again'.[28] Of their friendship Pat
would say: 'Dick wanted me as a friend for life rather than just
a one-night stand or a quick affair. I've always seen that as a
wonderful compliment.'[29] Shortly before her death Pat would
remember on camera: 'He talked marriage with me more than
once and then said – quite rightly, really – "Patty, the minute

we did it, it would fall to the ground." In a sense, this was a truism, I think. It wasn't worth it; no it wasn't worth the risk.'[30]

Pat enjoyed a lifelong and affectionate (albeit platonic) relationship with her frequent co-star Bob Monkhouse, and his love for her was clearly apparent in Pat's *This Is Your Life* tribute in 1978. Another close male friend was Desmond Rayner, the husband of television agony aunt Claire Rayner. Pat would often teasingly call him the boyfriend Claire had 'stolen' from her but it was a light-hearted remark and she remained friends with both Claire and Desmond, who lived nearby in Harrow, until the end of her life.

By staying single for her entire life Pat was by no means alone. Many of her female contemporaries never married and were perfectly happy to put their career before matrimony. Pat's dearest friend and confidante Irene Handl was a prime example of this and once said she had never found 'time' to marry. Another close friend, Peggy Mount, also remained single as did colleagues nearer in age, including Joan Sims and Fenella Fielding. Pat was aware that for some time she projected the image of a 'man-mad spinster' – especially in the 1970s when she often appeared as 'herself' in programmes such as *Celebrity Squares* – but while she didn't rule out the possibility of meeting 'Mr Right' and settling down to a 'happy and peaceful old age', she also made it known that she was not 'looking for any man'.[31] Although Pat rarely complained about being lonely, saying 'I just don't have time for that; I have plenty of friends, I write a lot, I write lots of letters mostly, and then, of course, there's the work,' there were inevitably times in her life when she did become overwhelmed by her personal life, as remembered by some of those closest to her.[32]

Summing up her thoughts on matrimony and the potential impact it could have had on her career Pat would say: 'I've never been wildly ambitious; I think if I'd been married, my career would have gone out of the window.'[33]

As a codicil to the subject of marriage, Pat would jokingly propose to me (despite a more than fifty-year age gap!) via one of her letters. On 29th February 2000, by Irish tradition known as Bachelor's Day or Ladies' Privilege, she would write in bold red ink 'WILL YOU MARRY ME?!!'[34]

4

'Gravy-ating'

'One of television's most constant joys'

As Britain moved towards the 'Swinging Sixties', the entertainment industry was rapidly changing. Music, film and television were all booming, and the kind of radio series in which Pat had made her name steadily became less and less popular. The transition from radio star to a household name on the small screen was a gradual one for Pat. She made the move seem effortless, despite the vast technical differences in performing in front of a camera rather than behind a micro-phone, but the changes in the industry were not always easy to navigate. Likewise, work was not always easy to secure.

As the medium of television grew beyond all recognition so too did Pat's list of credits. Irene Handl would often jokingly say that Pat 'gravy-ated' (rather than gravitated) from radio to the small screen. Although she always stated that her voice was her greatest talent, Pat's physicality was also ideally suited to television. She was distinctive-looking: tall, angular and often full of nervous energy. This frequently resulted in her playing 'mousy' characters – the downtrodden friend, the eternal spinster or the eccentric next-door neighbour. Happily Pat never seemed to tire of such roles.

Following her 'splendidly acted' appearance on the small screen in *The Old Curiosity Shop* in 1960 she was hailed as 'one of television's most constant joys'.[1] She made another well-received appearance alongside Libby Morris in *Saturday Spectaculars*, the production featuring numbers choreographed by Eleanor Fazan and scripts by Jimmy Grafton, Alan Fell and Jeremy Lloyd. Also in 1960 came *Leave it to the Boys* – written by Bob Monkhouse and Denis Goodwin – which saw Pat teamed again with Irene Handl. The hour-long show also featured the vocal group The Avons and guest artists including June Whitfield, Dick Bentley and Max Wall.

Despite a promising start to the decade, offers of work became few and far between and the early 1960s were a particularly 'dry' period for Pat as far as acting roles were concerned. The strikes within the business in 1962 saw her sending many letters to various contacts at the BBC hoping to secure work on the radio. In her typical self-effacing way she would enquire: 'Might there be an odd strange lady wanted?' Like many in the acting profession, aware of the unpredictable and somewhat fickle nature of the industry, she always had a fear that her latest acting role would be her last. Her correspondence became increasingly desperate, harking back almost to how tough things had been for her at the end of the 1940s. At times she became uncharacteristically despondent and in one letter admitted how close she came to quitting the profession altogether, writing 'I should have left it all behind months ago.' Her 'begging' circulars revealed that 'the Coombs has never had it so bad', and for a time at least Pat was often unemployed. She had a lifelong and unfulfilled ambition to be a member of the BBC's radio repertory company and wrote numerous letters at the time hoping to be accepted. Sadly this was never the case.

A welcome return to work came when she made a guest appearance in *The Face of Loyalty*, an episode of *Faces of Jim*, a series especially written for Jimmy Edwards by Frank Muir and Denis Norden. A guest appearance on *The Tommy Steele Show*, alongside Hugh Lloyd, Peter Hawkins and Una Stubbs, also proved to be a success.

Gradually things within the entertainment industry began to improve and once again Pat could label herself a jobbing actress. She considered her work with Bing Crosby on a 1963 television 'spectacular' to be one of the highlights of her career. Years later she would recall: 'I was a little waitress in an olde English tea shoppe' and admitted that she finished her scene in one take, before suddenly realising she was working with a legend.[2]

In 1965 she was reunited with Irene Handl in the television series *Barney is My Darling*, written especially for Bill Fraser by Marty Feldman and Barry Took (who had previously written Fraser's hit television series *The Army Game* and *Bootsie and Snudge*). Irene played Fraser's wife and the series was her first real foray into the world of sitcom, while Bill Fraser admitted at the time it was a chance for him to cast off the character of Snudge. Cast as Miss Habbitt, Irene's close friend and confidante, Pat appeared in four episodes of the comedy which unfortunately was not picked up for a second series. Over thirty years later Pat would admit with honesty that she had no memory of working on the short-lived production!

Beggar My Neighbour first appeared on screens as a pilot episode in May 1966. Two series and a Christmas special in the following year kept Pat busy before a third and final series in 1968. Regarded as a 'keeping up with the Joneses' sitcom, the series centred upon two sisters, Lana (Pat) and Rose (played by June Whitfield) living next door to each other in Larkworthy Road in north London with their respective husbands, Harry and Gerald (played by Reg Varney and Peter Jones). The success and popularity of the series saw it run to a total of twenty-two episodes (with Peter Jones leaving after the first series to be replaced by Desmond Walter-Ellis)

Writers at the time were keen to point out that Pat's role in the series marked a change in her career, with the *TV Times* observing: 'Her part as Reg Varney's overdressed and overbearing wife… was something of a break for her because she was on the "winning" side.'[3] The camaraderie on the set was a key feature of the series' success and it proved to be a significant assignment for both Pat and June Whitfield, who would say at the time: 'The great chance for funny actresses now is in these BBC situation comedy series, where you are not out there on your own. It's teamwork, especially in a tight foursome like *Beggar My Neighbour*.'[4]

All four actors in the programme would be household names for decades; Peter Jones had already been a television star as Mr Fenner in *The Rag Trade*, Reg Varney would become internationally famous as Stan Butler in *On the Buses* (1969-

73) and June Whitfield, the last survivor of the quartet, became a beloved national treasure, still active into her nineties, and awarded a damehood in 2017. Given such company, it is hardly surprising that Pat would remember *Beggar My Neighbour* as one of her favourite sitcoms.

It was during this time that Pat became good friends with June Whitfield, with whom she had first worked on radio in the 1950s.[5] It was a friendship that would last until Pat's death. The two great ladies of British comedy would spend many happy hours together, both on stage and off, and June (along with Roy Hudd) would work with Pat until the very end of her life. In 1995, during June's *This Is Your Life* tribute, Pat would recall staying at June's house (their 'writing moment') while they were working together on *Beggar My Neighbour* and drinking 'whate wane' with June and her husband Tim until 4am. They were later caught on the landing heading to their respective beds by the couple's seven-year-old daughter (the future actress Suzy Aitchison) who reprimanded them, hands on hips, saying, 'Excuse me, but are you getting up or coming to bed?' As Pat recalled it was a 'naughty but nice' memory.

Despite her work on television and radio since the end of the 1940s, Pat considered *Beggar My Neighbour* to be a turning point in her career, saying in 1972: 'Looking back, that's when it really got going. Before that I'd always done small cameo parts.'[6] She later revealed that she accepted the part with trepidation, but it proved worthy of her bravery:

> David Croft, the producer, phoned me one day and said he'd like me to appear in a *Comedy Playhouse* production, the one from which the *Beggar My Neighbour* series was to originate. 'It's not your usual thing,' he said. 'But I hope you'll agree to do it.' Well, I read the script

and my first instinct was to turn down the part. For me this was big stuff and I felt I hadn't the confidence to tackle it. But then I reasoned that if David had faith in me, I must have faith in myself. I took the part. I never for a moment regretted doing so.[7]

In 2020 Mike Sharland, who wrote the series along with Ken Hoare, would recall his time on the sitcom in detail:

Pat Coombs came into my life when Ken Hoare and I wrote a sitcom called *Beggar My Neighbour* in 1966 as a *Comedy Playhouse*. We had an idea. In those days you could pick up the phone to fellow writer and comedy advisor Frank Muir at the BBC Television Centre and get a meeting. We wanted to work for the BBC because we knew we could develop our idea and have a say in casting.

Beggar My Neighbour the sitcom was about two married sisters who lived next door to each other. Their husbands, Gerald Garvey and Harry Butt, worked in the same factory. Gerald was a poorly paid junior executive and Harry was a very high-earning fitter. The white-collar Garveys struggled to make ends meet while the blue-collar Butts lived off the fat of the land.

Frank immediately saw the possibilities not only as a *Comedy Playhouse* but as a long-running sitcom. Frank teamed us up with producer/director David Croft to make a pilot to be shown in the *Comedy Playhouse* series. David was closely related to me so we quickly arranged a meeting to fix dates and start to talk casting.

What made David very successful was a great visual sense and the ability to get the right casting mix which is an art and essential in sitcom. We had a solid script and we all knew the success of our *Comedy Playhouse* would rely on the right casting to deliver the laughs and clinch a series.

Ken and I had wanted to work with Peter Jones for some time. David agreed and Peter came aboard. Next David suggested the very popular Reg Varney, an old-time variety artist who was great at inventing business and using props. Reg was a rarity, he was instinctive with a great natural talent. June Whitfield was next, one of the most reliable laughter-makers. She could get a big laugh from a look. Next we struggled to come up with an actor to play Reg's wife.

The breakthrough came early one morning. David called up to say he had seen Pat Coombs. Of course Pat was a very experienced character actor. David had followed her career and was sure she was ready to star in a sitcom. Pat was booked.

I've always found the first day of rehearsal is nerve-racking and fraught. You don't really know if the casting choices you've made are the right choices and if the cast is going to gel as a team and get on. The first read-through of the script told Ken and I that Pat was the right choice. She was funny, knew where the laughs were. The rehearsal room soon filled with warmth and laughter.

The recording went well; Pat was the least known of the foursome but she was equal to the task. The studio audience took to her. The *Comedy Playhouse* was a success and a series was booked. We started to write the series knowing the strengths of the actors we now had.

Reg Varney had what he called a 'dicky jam-tart attack'. He survived. We survived.

We started to make the series. A bed was provided for Reg to lie on during rehearsal. The only person who lay on it and fell asleep was Peter Jones which Pat found hilarious.

Pat was nervous, in a positive way, because she suddenly realised she was one quarter of the show, one of four stars, and her fellow actors were firing on all cylinders.

The series aired and within a couple of weeks Pat began to be recognised in the street. That changed the dynamic in the studio. We were still recording and audiences loved her character.

From a writer's point of view, Pat was a joy to work with. She was naturally funny. Dinners after the show were a riot as Pat told stories punctuated by that infectious laugh.

We wrote three series and every recording was enjoyable – Pat was part of a wonderful team. We had great ratings and appreciation.

We could have gone on for many series but Frank had left and the BBC had changes of personnel. Ken and I and the cast were kept hanging around. Ken and I were offered a major deal with Yorkshire Television. By the time the BBC offered us a thirteen-show contract it was too late: we had signed with YTV and spent the next few years working happily out of Leeds.

> It was a pity we were unable to do more episodes of *Beggar My Neighbour* with Pat as we had plans for her character.
>
> Pat was always in demand and rightly so. Her contribution to comedy is far greater than people realise.[8]

Pat was well aware that no amount of professional success guaranteed work. One popular series did not necessarily lead to another and she was forced, once again, to 'sign on', admitting after *Beggar My Neighbour*: 'I had a terrible time when the programme finally ended. The labour exchange got sick of the sight of me and I outran my benefit.'[9]

Despite constant fears that she would 'never work again', by the end of the 1960s Pat was well established as a leading comedy actress on radio and television.[10] She had found her niche playing working-class characters: timid wives or friends, 'doormats', eccentrics and simpletons. In this position she was perfectly content. She had no desire to pursue a highbrow career on stage, as did her friend and co-star Peggy Mount (who in the 1980s became a celebrated member of the Royal Shakespeare Company), nor indeed to become a prolific film actress (in the vein of her contemporary Marianne Stone who made more than two hundred screen appearances over a period of forty years).

Actress and author Eleanor Bron worked with Pat on television and radio on a couple of occasions during the late 1960s and again in *Cucumber Castle* in 1970. Fifty years later she would share her thoughts on where Pat lay in the hierarchy of the business:

> Of course I remembered her and that we had worked together oh so long ago. My memory of her is dressed for performance, usually with a scarf tied around her hair and a cigarette dangled from her mouth,

playing a hard-done-by housewife or skivvy. I think the faintness of the recollections are in part due to the fact that we were not engaged in lengthy rehearsals as for a play, but in rather hasty preparations for brief sketches. These didn't call for a lot of probing or heart-searching, one way in which actors get to know each other. I have also a vague sense that on my part, two other factors weighed in, though not consciously: one a question of 'class' – in those days that was often a focus, sometimes submerged, of the satirical sword, but may nonetheless have been ingrained. Other classes were foreign countries to some extent; Pat may also have seemed much older perhaps than she was – another foreign place. In addition, I may have looked on Pat as a 'legitimate' actress, whereas I was still feeling that I had crashed into the profession, through the satire boom.[11]

Following the success of *Beggar My Neighbour*, Pat was teamed with Jimmy Edwards playing Mr and Mrs Croucher in *Don't Dilly Dally on the Way*, the fourth of six single productions in the series *The Galton and Simpson Comedy*. The plot centred upon the couple preparing to move from their bungalow of twenty-three years, but Mrs Croucher refuses and locks herself in the toilet. This appearance brought Pat into contact with the future *Carry On* star Jacki Piper, who remembered her colleague as 'very talented, very funny and so easy to work with', and David Jason, then at the beginning of his long career.[12]

In 1969 when Pat was appearing on television in *The Making of Peregrine*, with Dick Emery and Sam Kydd, journalist Ann Purser would sing her praises, writing: 'I must add a word about Pat Coombs, who keeps up a stream of appearances as funny ladies, never the same twice, never carelessly relying on one funny voice or portrayal that has been done before. Her acting is subtle and varied…'[13] Other appearances at the time included *Wild, Wild Women* which saw Pat playing Daisy (a role played in the series pilot by Penelope Keith), a garment worker in a milliner's shop in early Edwardian/suffragette England. Seen as a 'period piece variation on *The Rag Trade*' (the highly successful sitcom), it sadly failed to live longer than one series.[14] In between regular work on radio were a series of guest appearances and one-off roles including playing a traffic warden in *Meter Maids* in 1970, alongside Barbara Windsor and Joan Sanderson.[15]

A break with tradition for Pat came when she was cast as the 'simpering' Miss Tox in the 1969 BBC version of *Dombey and Son*, dramatised by Hugh Leonard. This was one of her very rare roles in a dramatic production, regarded at the time as an 'unaccustomed appearance'.[16] Based on the 1848 novel by Charles Dickens, the production featured, amongst others, John Carson (as Mr Dombey), Kara Wilson, William Moore, Fay Compton, Clive Swift, Davyd Harries, Charlotte Mitchell, and two episodes even saw the appearance of the future Dame Twiggy Lawson. Pat's role in five episodes of the series saw her teamed with Hilda Braid and proved her acting abilities were by no means limited to comic characters, although the change certainly did not alter her career in any way and it would be another three years before she would once again venture into the world of period drama.

Cucumber Castle, a medieval musical fantasy written by Barry and Maurice Gibb of the Bee Gees (who were also associate producers of the film), was an altogether more light-hearted production. Featuring Frankie Howerd (with whom Pat would later work in *Up Pompeii!*), Lulu, Julian Orchard, Spike Milligan and Vincent Price, the bizarre made-for-television film saw Pat playing the king's devoted nurse, Sarah

Childsbottom, and allowed her to revel in the silliness of high comedy.

As the decade ended Pat had much to be thankful for, and her reputation and success as an actress was shared by her family. Despite his initial concerns regarding his daughter's decision to become a full-time thespian, Thomas Coombs could now take pride in her achievements as a radio and television star. A new generation of family members also revelled in her fame, including her niece Sally Cryer, who would remember her aunt with fondness in 2020:

> Pat was always a big part of my childhood, and into my adulthood. Even though my parents were divorced when I was eleven years old, Pat remained great friends with her sister-in-law (my mother), and was a frequent visitor in our house, bringing fun and laughter with every visit. She took me to see rehearsals and shows, usually at the BBC, Shepherd's Bush, where I met many actors, enriching my life. When I was quite young, she took me to Hamley's toy shop and bought me a string puppet of Pinocchio. After, we went to her bedsit (Penny thinks it might have been in Swiss Cottage) for tea. The puppet was for my birthday and I loved it and played with it for years. I have memories of being in the bar at the BBC with Spike Milligan and meeting Bob Monkhouse, and many others.[17]

Pat's nephew Simon also embraced her connections with show business and would recall how his aunt's career brought him unforgettable experiences:

> I remember a few occasions that Aunt Pat would receive a special invitation to an elaborate gala event or awards ceremony. Since the invitation included a 'guest', I would accompany her to a few. One was held at the Waldorf Hotel, London. Dressed in my best suit possible, I would be in awe of the celebrities that knew Aunt Pat and who would chat with her. As a teenager, it was a cool experience to sit with her at a round table and be served an amazing meal while

being so close to famous people. I collected as many autographs as I could. Another award ceremony was held in a theatre. Sitting in rows among the famous was equally as exciting.

When I was about ten years of age, Aunt Pat and my entire family took a walkabout through Elstree Studios. There we met the Muppets and saw how the production came to be. This event took place while my family was on vacation to England prior to us moving back from Kingston, Ontario, Canada to Harrow, Middlesex.[18]

5

A stalwart stooge

'For an actress she's very modest and rather shy'

THE NINETEEN-SEVENTIES PROVED TO BE the busiest decade of Pat's long career. While the British film industry generally began a slow decline, television was booming and comedy sketch shows and situation comedies, for which Pat was ideally suited, were very much the flavour of the hour. For a great number of years Pat Coombs seemed to be everywhere; as the star of television comedies, a 'personality' on various game shows and as the voice of countless radio series and television commercials. It caused her to admit, very modestly, 'I've been rather lucky on television.'

During this time a large amount of Pat's income came via voice-over work. Her niece Penny Hey would recall that in the days of limited television channels, there was a time when almost every other advert was voiced by Pat. From perfume commercials (notably 'Just Musk', with her infamous catch-phrase 'Ooh-err, shouldn't be allowed'), to advertising both PG Tips and Typhoo tea bags ('You only get an oo with Typhoo') or fresh cream cakes, Pat's work in this medium was prolific.[1] Another niece, Tracy Lynch, even remembers Pat 'doing a celebrity stint on a freezer magazine called *Freezer Digest*, which I think is the original *Sainsbury's* magazine'.[2] Whilst others in the profession turned their noses up at 'commercial' work, deeming it beneath their dignity, Pat made the most of the genre and, ever conscious of earning a living for herself, was grateful for the financial rewards it offered.[3]

Pat's work in commercials even gained her an entry in *The Guinness Book of Records* for the greatest number of 'takes' (twenty-eight) for a commercial, as she would later reveal:

> Commercials are always hard work. They are so short, the timing just had to click. Well, we did 28 takes of my bit. The director, a nice patient man, was finally muttering about putting me up for *The Guinness Book of Records*. The trouble was that every time we came to the punchline I just couldn't remember the name of the product! That commercial has never been screened and come to think of it I've never seen the product in any shop. Which doesn't surprise me, really. Some kids who tried it couldn't eat it.[4]

In the early Seventies a string of appearances on the big screen also raised Pat's profile. She had made her film debut in the 1959 comedy *Follow a Star,* directed by Robert Asher. Hers was an uncredited role, as the 'simpering girl' in the theatre, and seemed to set the tone for future film appearances, which, by and large, were brief and often uncredited. Although she appeared in a dozen feature films it is fair to say that Pat was not a film actress – her niche was in radio and television and sadly the big screen undoubtedly failed to make use of her obvious talents. Too many of her film appearances were tiny, 'blink and you miss her' cameo roles.

One of her higher-profile (albeit still uncredited) film appearances was in the popular 1971 extravaganza *Willy Wonka and the Chocolate Factory*. Pat considered that she 'had a lovely part' as the north-country mother of the unforgettably awful Veruca Salt (played by Julie Dawn Cole) and wife of factory owner Mr Salt (played by her friend Roy Kinnear).[5] She would go on to feature in a more sizable part in the film version of *On the Buses*, opposite her old chum Reg Varney, in which she played one of a group of militant lady bus-drivers (alongside Pamela Cundell, Claire Davenport and Eunice Black) battling against male chauvinist colleagues. In 1972 her friendship with Dick Emery led to her playing his landlady and platonic girlfriend in *Ooh, You Are Awful*, a film very much designed to enable Emery to show off his talents to a wider audience.

While Pat's appearance in *Ooh, You Are Awful* was one of her more significant film appearances, in the same year she also starred in the short film *A Couple of Beauties* alongside James Beck (best known as Private Walker in *Dad's Army*) and also featuring Tim Barrett and comedian Bernard Manning. A Francis Searle production by Bayford Films of Shepperton, the film was labelled a 'comedy-thriller' and had been specially written for Bunny Lewis who was well regarded within the profession, having 'learned his craft alongside some of the all-time greats of the variety circuit and… topped the bill at the biggest venues in the UK'. The film centred upon a barman witnessing a murder in a London West End nighterie and subsequently disguising himself as a young woman to avoid the killers and escaping to Manchester to avoid being tracked down. Pat, successfully adopting a convincing north country accent once again, provided a strong supporting role in the little-seen production.

Sadly, entertainer and comedian Lewis did not achieve the 'national recognition he deserved' and *A Couple of Beauties* was not a success, mainly because of competition from higher-profile titles. As Patrick Nyland would write in Bunny's 2008 obituary: 'Timing is everything and unfortunately Bunny's film was overshadowed by the release of several movies on a similar theme that year by Frankie Howerd, Danny La Rue, Dick Emery and Reg Varney.'[6]

David Croft, who co-wrote *Dad's Army*, was well aware of Pat's skills and professionalism having worked with her in the past, so it was perhaps not surprising that she would feature (as Mrs Hall) in the film version of the popular television series, filmed in the summer of 1970 and released the following year. Her place in *Dad's Army* history was later secured when she featured in the 1975 radio series. Another more noteworthy film role came in *Adolf Hitler – My Part in his Downfall*, based on Spike Milligan's first volume of memoirs, in which she received decent billing, playing Spike's mother, Florence.

Key among Pat's film credits were her two appearances in the *Carry On* series. Produced by Peter Rogers and directed by Gerald Thomas, the immensely popular films began with *Carry On Sergeant* in 1958 and thirty more features would follow over the next twenty years. By the time Pat joined the cast more than a dozen of the popular comedies had been released, making stars out of the likes of Kenneth Williams, Sid James and Joan Sims. In *Carry On Doctor* she had a wordless cameo role as a hospital patient who asks Bernard Bresslaw (disguised as a nurse) for a bedpan and is somewhat surprised by the item she receives. Her role in *Carry On Again Doctor*, although equally brief, did at least give her a speaking part when she played the super-snooty new matron who tells Kenneth Williams (as Doctor Frederick Carver) to 'run along'.

Despite the brevity of her involvement in the *Carry On* films, Pat has forever been associated with the series. Having become such a familiar face in the world of comedy it was often assumed that she appeared in lots of the famous comedies, rather than just two. For her part, Pat was thrilled to be involved in the iconic classics writing in 1997: 'Working with the Carry On people I can only say my time(s) with them were very short – but I love each and every one! Tho' found Ken Williams a bit scary 'cos he was so outspoken.'[7]

Tantalisingly, Pat apparently missed out on another (unnamed) *Carry On* film when she suffered an accident while filming an advert for Yellow Pages; she was required to have mud thrown into her face as part of the commercial, which resulted in it accidentally going in her eyes and causing weeks of pain. She would later reveal: 'What specially disappointed me was that I was due to start in a *Carry On* film on the Monday and couldn't make it.'[8]

Arguably, Pat would have made an ideal member of the regular cast of unique *Carry On* actors who made the films their own. She had perfect comic timing, could play a variety of roles and would have been a suitable sidekick for the wonderfully eccentric Kenneth Williams or the equally zany Charles Hawtrey.

Despite her foray into the world of film-making in the early 1970s, radio and television remained Pat's main source of work and she was pleased to be cast in *Lollipop Loves Mr Mole* (later shortened to *Lollipop*), which ran for two series and a short Christmas special in 1971. Written by Jimmy Perry (famous for such classics as *Dad's Army*, *It Ain't Half Hot Mum* and *Hi-De-Hi!*), the series starred Peggy Mount and Hugh Lloyd as Maggie and Reg Robinson, a love-struck husband and wife whose pet names for each other were reflected in the series title. Pat played Hugh's sister-in-law Violet Robinson who returns to England with her husband Bruce (played by Rex Garner) from Africa to become long-term – and unwelcome – guests of Maggie and Reg.

Pat and Hugh Lloyd had been friends for many years having worked together on a number of occasions since the 1950s. In his autobiography, published in the year of Pat's death, he would describe her as 'a wonderful comedy actress, who to this day remains a good friend'. Hugh's relationship with Peggy, whom he regarded as formidable and 'larger-than-life', was sadly less affectionate.

Actor and writer Ian Masters, who toured with Peggy on stage in *The Mating Game* and wrote *It's Never Too Late*,[9] was close friends with Hugh Lloyd (who was best man for Ian when he married for a second time) and confirms that the relationship between Mount and Lloyd was not an easy one:

> Peggy was an interesting person – quite a mixture – quite private in lots of ways – quite puritanical – if she thought someone was being not quite 'good' or she'd heard rumours they'd been naughty or were having affairs on tour or things like that she was completely cold and she could completely snub people.
>
> Hugh Lloyd had a bad time with her during the rehearsals and he kept saying to me 'I don't know what I've done' and I said 'don't worry about it'. She used to get a bee in her bonnet that somebody

had done something out of her puritanical sphere as it were and she would strangely go really off you… poor Hugh was really upset because he didn't know what he'd done, but then she'd come round.[10]

Despite feeling that the first series was 'rubbish', Jimmy Perry was commissioned to write a further seven episodes by Bill Ward, head of ATV at the time, who was more than happy with the viewing figures of over 16 million; and the two veteran stars of the series managed to put aside personal differences to star in a total of thirteen episodes of the sitcom plus a short Christmas special.[11]

One episode of the series in particular stood out in Hugh's memory, so much so that he recalled it for Pat's *This Is Your Life* episode and in his memoirs:

One episode was filmed in a safari park where we got mixed up with some lions. Peggy and I had to film a scene were [sic] a lion cub had crept up behind us as we sat under a tree. Fortunately the trainer wasn't far away but another shot was done with Peggy and I and Pat and Rex all sitting inside a car in the park… with lions crawling all over it. There was no sound being recorded in the car, just the expressions on our faces and when it was screened we could clearly see Pat, in genuine terror, mouthing a four-letter word which would *not* have been acceptable on our screens 30 years ago![12]

*

By far the most devastating event of the 1970s for Pat was the death of her beloved mother, Hilda. The pair had been devoted to one another for over forty years when Hilda died at the King Edward VII Memorial Hospital, Haywards Heath, on 20th December 1971, aged seventy-three.[13] It was a loss from which Pat never fully recovered and especially poignant coming as it did just days before Christmas, a time of year Hilda had always loved. Although she was in her seventies and had been admitted to hospital with high blood pressure, Hilda's grand-daughter, Penny Hey, recalls, 'I didn't think it was anything serious... I certainly wasn't worried.' Hilda's sudden death from a heart attack occurred while Pat was working, as Penny explains: 'I remember Pat telling me she was driving back from filming/rehearsing and just knew that her mother had gone. They did have a very, very close relationship... It was just before Christmas and it really upset Pat to see the mince pies ready for Christmas in the tin.'[14]

Hilda was Pat's best friend, and whilst living with her parents Pat had felt supremely comfortable. It is possible that the warmth and security Pat felt at home held her back from seeking other relationships, although Hilda was a fun-loving and gregarious character and it is likely she would have taken great delight in Pat marrying and having a family. It was only after Hilda's death that Pat would really begin to experience times of loneliness and depression, to which only a few were privy.

A shared interest between Pat and Hilda was spiritualism and Hilda had long vowed that she would 'make contact from the other side' after her demise. Sometime after her death, Pat and Penny went to see the well-known spiritualist Doris Stokes; but, as Penny remembers, 'My grandmother didn't come through. I think if it had been possible, she would have managed it.'[15]

Work proved to be Pat's salvation and months after Hilda's death she would admit: 'Within a few days I found myself working on a Dick Emery show. I couldn't believe that I was able to do it. I suppose it was a kind of escape.'[16] Five years after Hilda's death Pat would concede that she almost 'went to pot' over her mother's death:

> We were very close. One knew it was going to happen, but you're still not really prepared and I wasn't nice to know for a long time afterwards.[17]

Pat had continued to live with her parents after they moved into a newly built bungalow near Hayward's Heath in Sussex while keeping on the handy little bedsit she had used in Swiss Cottage for years when working. Within ten months of Hilda's death her widower had remarried to Phyllis Everett: a twice-widowed seventy-four-year-old.[18]

Phyllis and Thomas had been childhood friends and reignited their relationship when she wrote to him after seeing Hilda's obituary notice. While Pat remained engulfed in grief for her deceased mother, her father's remarriage was some-what difficult to accept, although her relationship with Phyllis was always polite and civilised and she sensibly realised her stepmother brought companionship to her father in his old age. Pat had adored Hilda and it was clear to everyone that she could never be replaced in any way, shape or form in her daughter's eyes. Pat always remained grateful for the stability and love her parents brought to her life, and not long after her mother's death she would say: 'It is a good thing to have a background in this business... a bit of sanity and solidarity.'[19]

When Thomas and Phyllis moved to Walmer in Kent, Pat finally fled the nest and bought her first home: a one-bedroom ground-floor flat – number 5 Wendela Court, Harrow on the Hill – where she would remain happily for the next twenty-five years.

Pat's new home proved to be her haven. She regarded herself as 'obsessively tidy' and enjoyed her own company, although the telephone and writing pad were rarely far from hand.[20] Family members were her most frequent visitors and Penny Hey remembers:

> Pat was very tidy and organised in a sort of messy sort of way. She had what she called her 'Patty piles'… A place for everything but not necessarily out of sight. She often said it was the Virgo in her. She normally sat at her small dining table, on an upright dining chair with phone, fags and a Patty pile near to hand. It was facing the TV which she could watch while on the phone and writing letters. I got the impression the TV would go on around 4pm to watch her favourite programme *Countdown*. She also loved *Coronation Street* and *EastEnders* and keenly watched the news. She was a great one as you know for letter writing and also chatting on the phone, which as I have mentioned before, we did almost on a daily basis. Goodness knows what we talked about when I look back now. If I was out, she would leave a long chit chat message on my ansaphone, it was as if she hadn't noticed I was out. Ahhhhh memories.[21]

Despite her not inconsiderable income (by the mid 1970s she was earning more than she ever had) Pat remained frugal. With the exception of an endless supply of cigarettes, she had few extravagances and her home remained very simple as Penny explains:

> Her décor was plain. She wasn't fancy and wouldn't have wasted money on making it fancy or super duper comfortable. It served a purpose. I remember her talking about changing her curtains from winter ones to summer ones which is something I had never heard of before. I guess it was a throwback to days without central heating?
>
> What she would splash out on (tongue in cheek here) were her cats. She would 'spoil' them by often buying them fresh fish and cooking it for them. She had a special saucepan to cook it up for them.[22]

Pat's fondness for cats was well known and over the years she had a variety of long-lived feline companions, often named after characters she had played on radio or television. In later years a visiting reporter would meet three of her pets, Persil, Rudy and Mungo, and made note of Pat's 'spotlessly tidy flat' and her 'passions for Wagner and toast and marmalade'.[23]

Another great love was cigarettes. By the time she reached adulthood Pat, like many of her generation, was a confirmed smoker and remained so until her death. In 1972 the *TV Times* wrote: 'She smokes anything between 20 and 40 cigarettes a day though tells her doctor it is more like 10; hates the smell and the messy ashtrays but doesn't have a strong enough urge to stop.'[24] By the end of her life Pat was famous for her very long 'More' menthol cigarettes and was rarely without one in her hand.

Over time her health suffered drastically because of the habit, and noticeably her voice became deeper and raspier (accentuating her contagious and mischievous laugh), arguably because of smoking. Her slender figure may also have been helped by her addiction, and friend and colleague Georgina Moon would recall with bemusement: 'She smoked... and didn't eat!'[25] On a couple of occasions, as smoking became increasingly unfashionable and as her health declined, she did consider quitting the habit. Pam Valentine remembers Pat asking at the end of her life, 'Do you think I should give up smoking?' to which Pam sensibly replied, 'What's the point? You'd be so miserable.'[26]

Dabber Davis, who continued to see Pat socially over the years, remembers his late wife (a former nurse at St Mary's Paddington) constantly pleaded with Pat to stop smoking. The couple would visit Pat in hospital at the end of her life 'when she was having one of her bad turns' and Dabber remembers her saying, 'I've only set fire to the sheets twice!'[27]

Pat's other vice was her love of white wine. One of her favourite 'tipples' was 'Concorde' (a medium sweet white wine) but, as her niece remembers, in truth Pat enjoyed 'anything cheap – and low alcohol – because in her mind it would last longer!'[28] A glass or two of wine every day remained a key feature until the very end of her life, and she would happily admit she was very partial to a 'slightly sparkling (CHEAP!) white wino'.

From her childhood Pat had enjoyed spending time near the coast, and there exist photographs of the two Coombs sisters in their knitted swimming costumes in the 1930s. Very occasionally she would treat herself to a holiday abroad, especially in the 1980s. Despite her love of the sea, two of her nieces recall that Pat 'would only paddle in the sea... in her 1950s swimming costume – this was in the 80s!' This was another example of her thriftiness and also demonstrated that Pat's weight rarely increased throughout her adult life.[29]

Pat's interest in astrology and the afterlife was also well known and one of her favourite subjects. Although brought up in the Church of England, she would admit to being 'open minded... as most people in the theatre are'.[30] She would say in 1972:

> I've been interested in astrology since my school days. I think there is a great deal to it and am fascinated by books on it – though some I have read are beyond my comprehension. I once had a session with Maurice Woodruff. He told me things about my personal life which he couldn't have found out in the ordinary way. He was so accurate, I went all goose-pimply.[31]

Linked to her love of astrology, Pat was also a fan of psychic readings and was a natural choice of guest to appear in Tom O'Connor's quiz show, *The Zodiac Game*, in the mid 1980s, with Russell Grant, John Inman and Rustie Lee. Her interest in the 'stars' never left her and one of her key questions during the early stages of our friendship was to ask my star sign.

Another of Pat's great passions was writing letters. She lived in an age untouched by email or social media and letters were often the only means of communication with family members and friends. She was always quick to reply to fan mail; invariably, when she had time, letters received an immediate response. Being naturally frugal, Pat would often 'recycle' envelopes or notepaper, long before it was environmentally friendly to do so. Sometimes notes would be written on the back of letters sent to her; quite often she would cut down sheets of paper to send 'quick' responses and she always had her own personalised compliments slips to send thank-you notes to fans. A rare indulgence came at the end of her life when she had postage stamps printed bearing her face (taken from a 1997 publicity photograph). She would cheekily label them her 'show-off stamps'.

In the early 1970s she would discuss her passion for correspondence:

> I've always loved writing letters – I do about a dozen a week. That's family mail, plus notes to friends (I'm always the one who remembers birthdays, etc.) and then there are my half dozen or so pen pals, some of fifteen years' standing. It's a real joy to share interests – but I think pen pals should be a happy extra, never a substitute for other relationships.

While some of her eccentricities were revealed five years later:

I am a manic letter-writer. On a quiet day, when I've got nothing much else to do, I can easily write eight letters. And I do mean letters – not notes. I had a birthday yesterday and I had no less than 41 birthday cards, and inside most of the cards there was either a short note or a letter. So I'll soon be going through them with a toothcomb and sending my replies. I've got a sister in Canada so there's a real need to write long and newsy letters to her.

But I'm very naughty with my letter writing because I scribble on anything as long as it's neat and readable. And I'm a very neat lady. Years ago a pal gave me an enormous pile of coloured typing paper – pinks and yellows and so on – and I'm still using that for my letters. Friends say to me, 'You're doing well, why don't you get some decent notepaper?' I think my letter writing stems in a way from my other ambition which has been tucked away very far down because somehow it didn't seem as though I could cope with it – I wanted to be a journalist.[32]

Pat's handwriting was large, distinctive and clear. Her letters were filled with a multitude of exclamation marks, underlined words, capital letters, abbreviations and occasional slang. Her own voice leapt from the page making every letter or note highly personal and invariably entertaining.

Gaps between work meant that Pat often had time to devote to correspondence although at times she admitted to being overwhelmed by quite how many letters she had to write, saying, 'The bump on my writing finger is practically a bunion.'[33] Her Christmas card list was always a major task, numbering over 140 individuals even at the end of her life when many of her contemporaries had passed away. Penny Hey also remembers that 'Pat used to help delivering letters for the post office at Christmas… in the days you could dip in and out relatively easily on part-time work. It might have been just one Christmas; I just remember thinking it really funny.'[34]

Another of Pat's pleasures, as previously mentioned, was talking on the telephone. She was a natural 'chatterbox', interested in the lives of others. Her one-time agent, Richard Stone, would write that Anne Wright, one of his longest-serving members of staff, 'would talk for hours and hours to anyone with a problem. Bill Maynard, Nicholas Parsons, Pat Coombs each took up two hours of her every working day.'[35]

Television also filled some of her spare time and she enjoyed keeping up with the work of friends and contemporaries. In the early 1970s she was a fan of the Margaret Lockwood series *Justice* (having admired the glamorous actress's work from as early as the 1940s) and, loving anything to do with the law, she was also a fan of *Crown Court*, the long-running courtroom drama which aired from 1972 until 1984. A more surprising choice of television viewing for Pat was showjumping and she would say: 'I had a few riding lessons once and, while I'm not a great sports viewer, this programme really puts me on the edge of my seat.'

In 1977 she would give a rare insight into her private life:

I used to do a lot of reading but the habit faded away when I made the discovery I needed reading glasses – and that made me cross and frustrated. I've got the reading glasses now but it was odd how the habit faded a bit.

I watch the television but I hate seeing myself on it. I think most of us do. But I look because I feel I ought to and it has a sort of fatal fascination for me. I end up thinking 'what a silly woman'.

I watch *Celebrity Squares*, which is just about the only thing I do on the box which is the real me, and I can't bear seeing that, either. In fact, I think that's more embarrassing than watching myself playing someone else who isn't quite me.

Peggy asked me what I was doing when the first show in the new series [*You're Only Young Twice*] was going to be screened. 'Sitting in a corner watching by myself,' I said. She said she was having some friends round and invited me, too. But I don't think I could bear that. I sit and watch by myself unless it's with family, of course. I find it all so embarrassing.

I'm terrible at sewing and not much better at knitting. But I like housework and I'm quite a good cook. Plain food, nothing fancy. There were seven of us at home – my parents, my brother and sister and my grandparents – and my mother was hopeless at cooking. So the job was passed on to me. Really her cooking was a joke. Many times she made rice pudding – and it had no rice in it! [36]

Outside of the heady world of showbusiness Pat's everyday life was a relatively tranquil one. She had many friends, from various walks of life, and because she often took people on face value her associations tended to be quite mixed. Within the profession she was well liked and well loved, but generally speaking the majority of her friends were not thespians, although she remained lifelong friends with Irene Sutcliffe, Bob Monkhouse, Dick Emery and of course George Raistrick. She had a strong relationship with her sister, Pam, and her nieces and nephews, and for decades was very good friends with Anne Harvey.

Anne was the younger sister of Raymond Brooks, who years earlier had married Pam Coombs (Pat's younger sister). Pam and Raymond had four children and in November 1965 would emigrate to Canada. Sadly their marriage was not a success. When Pam eventually returned permanently to England in January 1980 she was divorced. Recalling the relationship between her two aunts, their niece Penny Hey would remember:

Pat loved her younger sister and was very protective of her. She generously paid for Pam's very nasty, drawn-out divorce in Canada and paid for her and her children to come to England. Pat gave up her small one-bed flat for them and moved into temporary accommodation in another flat in the block. Anne [Harvey] also put up a couple of the kids (I think). This was done for Pam and kids because they were family... There was never any presumption, smugness or the feeling that anything was owed.[37]

Given Pat's status as one of the country's best-known comedy actresses, it was somewhat surprising that her friendship with Anne Harvey remained secret, especially in 1971 when Anne's name was blazoned across newspapers after her husband Ernest James was killed by her lover, Alfred Edward Parrott.

Anne had married (Douglas) Ernest Howell James in 1957 and they had two children. Eleven years later, whilst working as a barmaid, she reportedly began an affair with Alfred Parrott. It proved to be an 'on and off affair... with frequent quarrels'. After a day of heavy drinking on 7th March 1971, Parrott (who at forty years of age was nine younger than Anne's husband) arrived at the James household and fatally shot Ernest in the alcove of his living room. Parrott would later claim that the shotgun he was carrying had gone off accidentally, although at the time of his arrest he would tell police: 'I went there to kill him and I have done it and now she will be happy.'

Parrott's subsequent trial revealed his previous criminal record, with a number of convictions including one for assault in 1962. He had also been a patient in Shenley Mental Hospital in 1960. Passing sentence on the case, Mr Justice Stevenson would say: 'This is a sordid story of sex and alcohol. I do not forget that a measure of responsibility for your trouble lies on the shoulder of Mrs James with whom you consorted, but I cannot overlook the fact that you killed. On that night you set out with the equipment at least for doing serious injury and you are no fool with a gun'. Parrot was found guilty of man-slaughter on substantially diminished grounds and sentenced to six years in prison for killing his mistress's husband.[38]

Anne went on to marry again, to a much older former fiancé, who later died suddenly after inheriting both his mother and spinster sister's estates. She also worked at the BBC for a time, and was a key figure in Pat's later years and a beneficiary in Pat's will.[39]

Behind closed doors, in light of Anne's unfortunate marriage record, Pat would sometimes refer to her as 'the black widow'; yet her relationship with Anne was somewhat typical of her way of taking people on face value. In the words of her niece, 'Pat was too gullible and would easily have been taken in. She liked people and trusted them as a rule.'[40] She was indeed very innocent, almost to the point of being naive, and as a result was certainly taken advantage of in financial matters on more than one occasion. While her friendship with Anne was re-membered by some as a close one, and Anne was especially accommodating in Pat's final years at helping out with practical matters such as shopping and running errands, it was also an association that could potentially have seen Pat at the centre of many unsavoury (and career-damaging) newspaper headlines.

Pat's disappointment at never having her own children did not prevent her from becoming a loving and generous aunt to three nephews and four nieces. Always nurturing, she tried her best to support her family in whatever way she could. When her niece Penny thought about becoming an actress, Pat was encouraging, despite being all too aware of the ups and downs of the profession. Sending Penny a copy of Frieda Hodgson's obituary notice, she would write on the back: 'I think it will encourage your POTENTIAL!! Yer see – it's true (reading about Frieda) 'tis never too late to start!!'[41]

Her nephew Simon Brooks would remember that 'Aunt Pat had amazing family values' and looks back on his formative years, in which Pat featured heavily, with happiness:

> I remember my teen years in England well and they include fond memories of her presence. Birthdays, special holidays, Christmas time were always inclusive of Aunt Pat. At Christmas, her gifts were laid under the tree before Christmas morning. She would arrive to our home in time for gift opening and stay for a late lunch. She had her favourite treats that she was particularly fond of and that would be a box of Pot of Gold chocolates and Liquorice Allsorts. She was safe to enjoy the dark chocolates as she knew none of us kids would go near the stuff. She did particularly enjoy dark chocolate. Aunt Pat was very kind and generous to my mother (her sister). Although Aunt Pat had her own flat, she would often be at our rowhouse[1] when my brother, sisters, and I returned from a day at school. She would hang out with us until mother arrived home from work – chat a bit with her and then be on her way. She enjoyed returning home to her cats and her favourite meal of bangers and mash.
>
> As a young adult, when I was toying with the idea of staying in England or returning to Canada, Aunt Pat saw an entrepreneur side to me. She encouraged me to stay in England and set up business. She was very convincing; however, in the end the pull to return to Canada was greater. I left behind my dear Aunt Pat but carry her values within me.[42]

Public recognition was an occupational hazard of Pat's job. As early as 1955 she was making 'public appearances', yet she never craved attention. Although she had an instinctive ability

---

[1] In the US and Canada, a term for what in the UK would be called a terraced house.

to connect with people of all ages, and was well known for her talkative nature, Pat always shied away from the spotlight. 'For an actress she's very modest and rather shy. She'd rather run a mile than be collared by her fans,' said Tom Coombs in 1978. By the mid 1970s she was one of the best-known faces on television but would admit: 'The very word "star" makes me go hot with embarrassment if anyone thinks of applying it to me. I find it a frightening word.'[43] Signing autographs and posing for photographs with fans was something Pat accepted with her natural grace and patience, since she was well aware that fame inevitably brought some restrictions although she was often able to go about her day-to-day life unrecognised. She would recount in one interview that during the filming of *Beggar My Neighbour* a ten-year-old girl followed her around Hayward's Heath Library for several minutes before turning to her mother and saying, 'That lady was on television last night.' The mother of the child then 'looked Pat Coombs slowly up and down, taking in the dilapidated anorak and said, in a voice all stockbroker Tudor and cocktails on the patio: "Oh, I shouldn't think so dear!"'[44] Years later producer Steve Doherty would remember how good Pat was at spending time with fans at Broadcasting House although he felt she preferred the disguise of being 'in character' rather than being herself, a common trait for many in the acting profession.[45]

Pat's 'celebrity' status also impacted on her younger relatives, happily in a positive way, as her nephew Simon would explain:

Having an Aunt as a famous person made me a celebrity in some small ways. I remember going to Shaftesbury Circle after Whitmore High School. On occasion, Aunt Pat would be there shopping at Shaftesbury Pharmacy or the butcher's. My buddies would excitedly

say, 'Isn't that Pat?' I would go up to Aunt Pat and talk to her. My
buddies would say, 'You know HER?' I was very proud to tell them
that she was my Aunt. It amazed me how popular she was. Some of
my buddies would take time and ask for her autograph.[46]

Pat's work for charity began in the 1950s. A naturally kind
and generous person, she was always happy to help a good
cause, both publicly and privately. Although not especially
sociable – she invariably preferred to be at home with her cats
than sipping champagne with celebrities – she made countless
appearances at summer fetes, local bazaars, fashion shows,
galas and festivals. Animal charities were always her weakness
and, at the time of her seventieth birthday in 1996, she
requested that guests invited to her party should make a cash
donation to Mayhew House, a London-based animal welfare
charity for cats and dogs whose patron is now the Duchess of
Sussex. Numerous other charity groups benefited from her
support including the Cats Protection League, the National
Animal Welfare Trust (NAWT) and the Motor Neurone
Disease Association. In later years Help the Aged, the National
Osteoporosis Society and Meals on Wheels also enlisted her
support. Ironically in her old age she herself would benefit
from the services of good causes and in the late 1990s, when
she was often bedridden, Pat would admit: 'When I was unwell,
I couldn't cook, and I relied on the friendly meals-on-wheels
service for a healthy diet and company. Being housebound is
not fun and the driver always managed to boost my morale.'[47]

Three years after her appearance in *Dombey and Son*, Pat's
role in the 1972 BBC television adaptation of *Cranford* was
another rare dramatic appearance; and, although she often
stated that she had no real desire to be considered a serious

'straight' actress, the opportunity to play the village gossip Miss Pole, 'a marvellously sad/funny part', proved to be one of her personal favourites and a highlight of her career. She would say at the time:

> It was a real hen party at rehearsals. It got to the stage where we really began to look forward to a gentleman coming along to join us. Still, it's a good chance for the ladies to come into their own… the ladies of Cranford rule the village like Amazons. God help any poor man who comes along. But at the same time they are rather sad, all so poor and so nice and so genteel. It's funny and sad at the same time.[48]

The role brought many favourable reviews, from both critics and fans alike. A letter of support, preserved in Pat's scrapbooks, came from a Doctor Laurance Barclay, who wrote:

> I send you my sincere congratulations for your fine performance in the recent BBC production of *Cranford*. Your characterisation was a tour de force of artistry and technique. Not a part which seizes public imagination, perhaps, but one upon which you lavished skill which afforded me many delighted moments.[49]

In the same year, as Pat celebrated twenty-five years as an actress, she was busier than ever. In one weekend alone she was seen on television not only in *Cranford*, but also in *The Reg Varney Revue* and with Ken Dodd on both television and radio. In the same year she co-starred in the sitcom *Lollipop*, featured in numerous episodes of *The Dick Emery Show* and his feature film *Ooh, You Are Awful*, and was also working on radio in *The Things*.

Despite her prolific workload Pat remained very modest. A decade after almost quitting the business she was thankful for the spate of offers which had come her way, saying, 'I just can't think what has brought it all on.'[50]

Journalist Alec McKinty was under no illusion that Pat's 'pure talent' kept her in work and was especially impressed with her performance in *Cranford*, writing:

> *Cranford*, though, is a revelation. As the spinsterly Miss Pole Pat Coombs is demonstrating unsuspected depths. Miss Pole is a lonely, sad woman, lost in her fantasies and consumed with imagined romances. Yet she is a good-hearted, likeable and undramatic person. Miss Coombs has brought her complex nature to life with delicacy and feeling – though at first the part 'frightened her stiff'.[51]

Throughout the 1970s one of Pat's most constant joys was her work with Dick Emery in his television sketch show. They made more than forty appearances together on the small screen and Pat proved to be the perfect 'foil' for the master of mirth. In the early 1960s Emery had often called upon the talents of Joan Sims, who appeared in more than a dozen episodes of his television series, and other leading ladies including Una Stubbs and Mary Millar would also support him. It was Pat however who became the female mainstay of Emery's series, and she was always delighted to appear alongside her old chum. The long-running series also brought Pat into contact with Dabber Davis, who wrote for the show, especially on anything 'topical', and provided Dick with his legendary catchphrase, 'Ooh, you are awful!'[52]

Emery had a 'naughty but nice' schoolboy sense of humour which suited Pat perfectly. She in turn was an absolute professional who could (and did) take on a variety of character roles in his highly popular series and never failed to deliver superb performances. On the set Pat was guaranteed to bring happiness. Chatty, animated and self-effacing, she was loved by cast and crew alike and became Emery's ultimate stooge.

Her ability to keep people amused was a natural gift, one that was demonstrated not only professionally but also privately, as her nephew Simon Brooks remembers:

> Aunt Pat had an amazing sense of humour. Not only on screen but also in real life. I recall my 17th birthday and Aunt Pat thought she would pull a fun one. Prior to my birthday she asked me what I would like for my special day. I replied that a car would be nice – perhaps a red Ferrari. I neglected to mention the size I wished the Ferrari to be. True to her famous sense of humour, on my birthday she presented me with a key ring that had the word Ferrari on it. I was then handed a small box which I thought would hold the key to the new car. Opening it with a sense of anticipation, I roared with laughter when I saw the package didn't hold a key but instead was a very small red Matchbox Ferrari. Aunt Pat was hysterical with laughter. I was not disappointed. I valued her sense of humour and thought laughter was the best gift she could have given me.
>
> She also loved to mimic voices of other people when recalling a story. It added a great deal of comic relief to hear the many different voices that could come out of a rather sweet lady. She would take pleasure in trying to mimic our voices. It would be frustrating as a teen... especially since we were trying to be taken seriously. In the end, she would have us in a fit of laughter.[53]

As a relatively late starter to the profession it is interesting to note that Pat's age was frequently misreported and as a result for some time she was able to play characters much younger than her real age. For years, numerous sources stated that she was born in 1930, although she admitted in April 1972: 'I'm 45. Isn't it sickening? I don't believe it and don't feel it. But it's not a happy feeling getting old. Nobody really wants it. Thirty was a good point for me. After 40 you're dropping down the other side.'[54] The early years of youthful casting quickly disappeared, however, and by the time she reached her forties Pat was often seen as distinctly middle-aged characters or indeed as women much older than she actually was. She took the change in her stride, and for many television viewers she was one of those character comediennes who had always appeared 'middle-aged'. Despite her honesty about her age it was not until the 1990s that her true year of birth began to be reported.

In 1974 Pat would star in another television series, sadly now remembered as probably the worst sitcom of her career. *Don't Drink the Water*, written by Ronald Wolfe and Ronald Chesney, was seen as a follow-up to their hugely successful series *On the Buses* (which ran for over seventy episodes and included three spin-off films) and a chance for Stephen Lewis, who had previously played Blakey the gormless inspector in *On the Buses*, to resurrect his most famous character, now retired and having moved to Spain with his spinster sister Dorothy Blake, played by Pat.

Although the character of Blakey had been very popular, *Don't Drink the Water* was not well received. Johnny Mack wrote a long and detailed review, panning both the concept and the script. Only the performances of Pat and Derek Griffiths escaped his criticism. He wrote:

> … the situation was never believable… the inspector [Stephen Lewis] is just not strong enough to build a series around… he certainly seems out of place in a Spanish flat. His spinster sister (Pat Coombs) is her usual delightful 'ninny' but could benefit from a more imaginative script. Derek Griffiths, overcoming the deficiencies of the script, gives his usual sparkling performance. Casting him as the porter is one of the more enterprising aspects of the series… on the whole however the series is disappointing… altogether too hackneyed with too many clichés and too predictable.

Pat's main memory of *Don't Drink the Water* was the endearingly awful hairstyle she had to endure. Pat's character was originally fitted with a wig, although she later admitted: 'It looked too much like a wig so they gave me an authentic "Marcel finger-wave" – a horrific style that's been dead since the Thirties.' As a lady who was always keen to look her best, and as someone who had her hair 'set' on a weekly basis, Pat took great delight in returning her appearance to normal – as did her hairdresser – with Pat saying, 'It's odd, but when I go to the hairdresser he doesn't despair that his creation is going to be destroyed the next day. He feels he's done his bit.'[55]

Derek Griffiths was at the start of his career when he played Carlos the Spanish porter in all thirteen episodes of the sitcom. He would recall his happy memories of his co-star in 2019:

I worked with Pattie early on in my career in *Don't Drink the Water* for ITV. I remember Pattie with deep, deep affection. She was a very funny lady on and off the screen and completely and deliciously down to earth. We giggled like schoolkids together and we both had a weakness for their humour.

One week during rehearsals she had a prolonged tummy upset and was always dashing to the loo, much to the annoyance of our stern director Mark Stewart.

Next morning, she was thirty minutes late arriving; she rushed into the room in a fluster, apologising profusely.

'You are very late. WHY?'

She said, 'I was at the bus stop and I had to run all the way home again. I was just in time.'

'In time for what?' Mark Stewart asked.

'Another tin of soup!'

He wasn't quite sure and decided not to ask. I was helpless, on the floor, and was immediately shouted at.

Another time, we were doing a camera rehearsal in the studio; things were tense as we were behind the morning schedule and the lunch break was looming very near. I was outside the door awaiting my cue to enter, when one of the camera crew broke wind, loudly.

Pattie, mid speech, ground to a halt and spluttered giggling. Mark Stewart's voice boomed over the tannoy 'Keep going!' Pattie tried but was wheezing, laughing and coughing all at the same time. The studio door burst open and Mr Stewart marched on to the set: 'WHAT IS SO FUNNY?'

Pattie, crying and red-faced, said, 'Someone farted.'

Stewart: 'And what is so funny about a fart?'

Pattie: 'It comes from such a funny place…'

The studio broke up laughing and that last line has been with me for over forty years. She was loved and adored by all… even Mark Stewart.[56]

Amazingly, despite being described as 'one of the most excruciatingly poor ITV sitcoms of them all', *Don't Drink the Water* ran for two series. It was later released onto DVD.[57]

A personal highlight in Pat's career was the opportunity to work with Sir Paul McCartney on a part-animated concert film: Paul McCartney's *The Bruce McMouse Show*. The production was directed by Barry Chattington and told the story of 'how Paul McCartney and Wings came to meet the inimitable impresario Bruce McMouse'. The animated portion of the film featured the voices of Paul and Linda McCartney, Deryck Guyler, Derek Nimmo and Pat (as one of the mice) and was recorded at the end of 1973.[58] Around the same time she was also pleased to be reunited with her *Beggar My Neighbour* co-star, Reg Varney, in numerous episodes of his television series.

A further sitcom in 1976 saw Pat playing the Scottish housekeeper Mrs Mac in series two of the children's comedy *Hogg's Back*, starring Derek Royle as the absent-minded Dr. Hogg. Written by Michael Pertwee (the brother of *Doctor Who* and *Worzel Gummidge* star, Jon Pertwee), the series saw Royle supported by a wide range of guest actors including Arnold Ridley and Hugh Lloyd. In the same year she was at Elstree Studios dressed as a 'bulging budgie' as a guest star in Marti Caine's television series – the antics of these 'two long, thin women… wobbling about in costumes, flapping their wings and squawking "Who's a pretty boy then?" was a sight that had the blasé camera crews doubled up with laughter'.[59]

After avoiding work in the theatre for almost two decades, Pat returned to the stage in 1976 in *Emu in Pantoland* at the Shaftesbury Theatre. Resurrecting her character of Nola from *Hello Playmates*, she joined Irene Handl to star alongside Rod Hull and his famous 'Emu' puppet. The show was described as 'the first entirely original production to be presented to the West End in fifty years'.[60] Co-stars in the panto included Victor Spinetti, Susan Maughan, Bob Todd and Carl Wayne.

Irene Handl had remained a constant presence in British theatres since her stage debut in 1937. She had also appeared in numerous pantomime productions and it seems likely her friendship with Pat led to her persuading 'Nola' to return to tread the boards once again. The production also led to a 'naughty but nice' anecdote, which was often repeated by Pat:

> Classic Irene H. remark… We were called to Emu's dad (Rod Hull) for notes on the panto… Rod was with his wife – but stark NAKED doing up his shoes!! We collapsed when we came out and Irene said 'Pat dear, did you <u>see</u> it? It was the size of a walnut!!!'

After writing this, Pat also cheekily commented, 'I dare you to print that!?' and later admitted 'I'm grateful Irene said it and not me!!'[61]

Perhaps buoyed by her return to stage work, in the spring of 1977 Pat travelled to Guernsey to take part in an all-star charity show (arranged by Dabber Davis) which featured a variety of artists including David Jacobs, Wei Wei Wong and Frank Bough. The event, organised to raise funds for the Chest and Heart Association, allowed Pat not only the opportunity to perform in front of a live audience but also gave her the chance to experience the beauty of the island.

A less publicised role from 1976 onwards was Pat's work with the Samaritans. After taking a six-week 'crash course' on how to handle calls from desperate people with urgent problems, she often spent entire nights listening to those in need. Her callers, of course, were initially unaware that they were speaking to a famous actress. To them she was simply 'Pat' – a friendly voice at the other end of a telephone, prepared to listen to a variety of problems, from potential suicides to unpaid bills. On her decision to join the Samaritans Pat would say: 'I have time to give to others. Missing out on marriage was my own doing, but one can't spend the rest of one's life moping. While one can continue laughing and being fairly cheerful, one will always have friends.'[62]

Almost inevitably when word 'got out' that Pat Coombs was working for the Samaritans they received quite a number of calls specifically requesting to speak to her. She later became less vocal about her involvement with the charity, saying in 1979: 'It's not something I want to talk about. The whole essence of this work is to be anonymous.'

Within the business, Pat's involvement with the Samaritans caused some bemusement as her colleague Chris Emmett would recall:

During the ten-year run of Yorkshire Television's *3-2-1*, whenever Pat was a guest on the show we would both be staying at the Queen's

Hotel in Leeds and you could guarantee that late at night when, inevitably, as I was going over my lines for the next day, Pat would ring me on the house phone for a brief chat – '...a quick catch-up,' she called it. Brief? I was lucky to get to bed before 2 o'clock! My God could Pat talk! It was during one of these conversations that she suddenly told me that she was a volunteer for the Samaritans. I joked, immediately, 'Samaritans? What do you tell them, apart from come out with the classic Nola line, "'Ere, why don't you stick your nose in your ear and blow your brains out?"' She burst out laughing and then said, 'No, I'm deadly serious.' After further incredulous questioning from me I said, 'Why do you do it?' and she replied, 'I'm a good listener and I enjoy talking.' (Ye gods, I knew that!) To this day I have no idea if she was pulling my leg or telling me the truth but I still find it difficult to imagine this bright, perennially perky woman talking down potential suicides.[63]

A spate of guest appearances on television led to Pat being asked to appear on *Celebrity Squares*, the popular game show hosted by her old friend Bob Monkhouse from 1975 to 1979. She accepted the offer with some trepidation, admitting:

I'm rather a shy person. I'm used to hiding behind a silly hat and voice and bouncing lines off other characters. In programmes like *Celebrity Squares* you are on your own. It was quite, quite scarifying.[64]

Pat's appearances on *Celebrity Squares* brought her a new fan base, although at the time she was surprised to be asked back for more episodes, saying, 'I don't think I got one answer right. I was amazed when the producer asked me to fix up another appointment.'[65]

She was aware that television viewers initially thought she was imitating Angela Rippon's voice, since they had rarely heard the 'real' Pat; yet despite her initial fears, she loved appearing on the show which also brought her into contact with many old friends and colleagues including Diana Dors,

Roy Kinnear and Larry Grayson. It boosted her confidence in some ways too, as she also revealed:

> I still don't like doing jobs without a script. But it was *Celebrity Squares* which finally taught me how to relax, and be myself. Even now though I can't open bazaars or give an impromptu speech. If they stick me on a long table, with the white tablecloth, a vase of flowers and the Mayor and Mayoress and all that, I go to pieces. I just can't do it. I get in a terrible state. I couldn't give a speech to save my life. I'd die of panic.[66]

Following on from *Celebrity Squares* Pat gradually began to appear on more and more quiz shows, notably *Blankety Blank*. As well as keeping her in the public domain such programmes even brought about new friendships with contestants: not least with Scottish vet Mrs Pat Morris, who remembered Pat in 2020:

> I first met Patti in Elstree Studios… I was a contestant in *Celebrity Squares*, hosted by Bob Monkhouse, and although Pat wasn't in the edition I took part in I met her in the studio area and we got chatting.
>
> When she found out I was a vet we got talking. Patti was very much a 'cat' person, and had a British Blue kitten, called Buzby after the telephone advert she had done. We talked and talked – and when I told her my hobby was photographing pets she immediately asked if I would take some photos of Buzby for her.
>
> I was going down to London in a few months for a vet conference and staying for a few days so we agreed that I would visit her in her home in Harrow – 5 Wendela Court! The conference was in the centre of London and so I got a train out to Harrow.
>
> Patti as always was warm and friendly and Buzby was adorable. I took lots of photos for her – and sent them all to her – and sadly have none myself now. She was charming and elegant and nothing like the downtrodden spinsterish characters she often portrayed. She took me to meet her sister Pam who lived nearby and her niece Sarah – who was then working in Harrods I think – and nephew Wilfred. They had two dogs as I recall!

It was a lovely day and I enjoyed it very much. Patti had a super sense of fun, and we got on very well.

After I got home, we kept in touch weekly. One or other of us would phone and we'd have long chats. She was a superb mimic and I never quite knew who was phoning me – she could imitate so many well-known TV stars – and we had many a laugh. Her osteoporosis wasn't great but she was thrilled to tell me she was delighted with a new car she had bought – a Ford Ka – a very small car for a tall lady, but she said it was perfect for her.

She told me all about an osteoporosis 'do' she had attended; she had sneaked off into a side room for a cigarette and found another lady there having a crafty cigarette – Camilla, later to become married to Prince Charles. She told me Camilla was such fun and a lovely lady. Patti (like me at that time) was quite a heavy smoker, which contributed eventually to her emphysema. She told me about some of the romances she had when a bit younger and she said she had nearly got married twice – in fact, I think she was engaged, but not sure.[67]

One of Pat's more unconventional appearances in the latter half of the 1970s was her performance as Miss Spider in a BBC adaptation of the Roald Dahl children's classic, *James and the Giant Peach*. Her colleague in the production, actress Kate Lock, would recall the slightly bizarre experience:

Pat was great fun and a good laugh on and off the set of *James and the Giant Peach*. I was much younger and unknown amongst a cast of celebrity actors, playing the Ladybird to Pat's Spider. She was, I remember, very kind and friendly to me, and I was slightly in awe of my fellow thesps at the time. We were all 'imprisoned' in amazing outfits befitting our insect/animal life and Pat found it all very amusing. She seemed very fond of Hugh Lloyd and they would giggle together about the 'old' days. Bernard Cribbins was very much the centre of attention but Pat got along with everyone.[68]

Two years later she was again in costume, playing the Dormouse, in an *Alice in Wonderland* sketch in *Have A Harry*

Birthday, a Yorkshire Television production especially written for ex-Goon Harry Secombe by Barry Cryer, Spike Mullins and Peter Vincent. Radio work also continued to keep her busy, not least appearing with Richard Beckinsale, the star of popular television series including *Porridge* and *Rising Damp*, in two series of *Albert and Me*. Jim Eldridge, who wrote the series, would recollect Pat and their association in 2020:

I can't remember the actual date I first met and worked with the wonderful Pat Coombs, but I know it must have been either late in 1971 or early 1972, because the episode of my Radio 2 sitcom, *Parsley Sidings*, in which she guest-starred was first broadcast in January 1972.

Parsley Sidings (produced by the legendary Edward Taylor) was set in a small rural railway station and starred Arthur Lowe as Horace Hepplewhite, the stationmaster; Kenneth Connor as Percy Valentine, the station's devious porter, and also Bradshaw, the ancient signalman, as well as various other voices (including Clara the station hen); Liz Fraser as Gloria, the timetable announcer; and Ian Lavender as Horace's gormless son, Bert Hepplewhite, the booking clerk. Pat came in for Episode 8 of the first series, titled 'Who'll Be Mother'. She played Horace's absent-minded sister, Maude Smallpiece, and also her baby son, Cyril. The story is that when she boards the train, she forgets to take her infant son, and the station staff are left with the responsibility of looking after baby Cyril until Maude returns to reclaim him.

Pat was brilliant in both parts, but especially as baby Cyril, with no actual words to say, just baby noises which she used to express happiness, misery, disgust (great raspberry-blowing!), hunger, everything. The skill of creating comedy with just sounds and gibberish and no actual words, and making an audience roar with laughter, is a very rare talent. The only other person I saw do it with equal skill was Kenneth Connor when he played the aforementioned station hen having an in-depth conversation with stationmaster Horace. The playing of this scene between Arthur and Ken was a masterclass in radio comedy, with Ken's variety of hen noises having the studio audience rolling in the aisles. Equally, Pat was so brilliant as baby Cyril that the audience at home could 'see' the baby and the chaos looking after it caused, especially to the uptight Horace.

Fast forward to 1976: I'd just sold a new sitcom to BBC Radio 2 called *Albert and Me*. It was about a single-parent father, Bryan Archer (played by Richard Beckinsale), bringing up his baby son, Albert, and was inspired by the fact that at this time I was also a single-parent father bringing up his young son. For this series I was working with a different producer, John Fawcett Wilson, who I'd already worked with on Ronnie Barker's *Lines From My Grandfather's Forehead* and the thriller *Down Payment on Death*. When we discussed who could play baby Albert, I reminded him how brilliant Pat had been playing a baby in *Parsley Sidings*. John pointed out that if we had Pat in what would now be a series, we needed to give her more to do than just make baby noises, and said what a brilliant and versatile actress she was (which I was already aware of). And so I created the part of Bryan's mother for her.

Watching (and listening to) Pat and Richard work together was a delight. The audiences thought so, too, and we were all set to make a second series when tragically Richard died at a very young age, and so, too, did the series. At least, that's what we thought. John Fawcett Wilson and I then went on to create a different and much broader comedy series, *Tony's*, set in a hairdressers, starring Victor Spinetti, John Laurie (with Deryck Guyler in the second series after John sadly died) and Deborah Watling.

In 1980 a new Controller of Radio told the Head of Comedy: 'I want more thoughtful comedy. Why don't we bring back *Albert and Me*, with a new star?'

John Fawcett Wilson and I jumped at it. We'd loved doing the first series, and the chance of working with Pat again was not to be missed. For the new series we had Robert Lindsay taking over the part of Bryan, with Pat once again playing Bryan's mother and baby Albert. Again, the audience loved it, and there would have been more, but Robert had decided to move into other areas. But I was grateful for what we'd had.

For me, my overriding memory of Pat is her gentleness, her kindness, her generosity as a performer (and a person). I have worked with some 'stars' who act in that pain-in-the-arse 'starry way', eager to grab the best lines, and determine to be The Important One. Pat was the antithesis of this: low-profile, always genuinely pleasant to everyone, whether cast, crew, tea-lady, everybody. As a result, everyone adored Pat.

Sadly, our paths went in different directions after *Albert and Me*, but that is the nature of showbiz. But I will always have those fond memories, especially when I hear *Albert and Me* rerun on radio, and think how fortunate I was to work with such a wonderful, talented and skilled artiste.[69]

6

A Lifetime of comedy

'Everybody loved her and you can't say that about many people'

THE MUCH CELEBRATED SILVER JUBILEE of Queen Elizabeth II in 1977 also marked the twenty-fifth anniversary of Pat's television debut. At the time she admitted that although she had often played 'doormats' she was also grateful for the professional opportunities she had enjoyed, saying, 'I've made a very good career out of it.'[1] Further success would follow in another long-running sitcom for which she was ideally cast.

Yorkshire Television's *You're Only Young Twice*, starring Pat and Peggy Mount, ran for thirty-one episodes (four series and two Christmas specials) and brought the pair another major hit on the small screen. The series was set in Paradise Lodge, a large detached house for 'retired gentlefolk', and centred upon the antics of four of its residents, played by Peggy (as Flora Petty), Pat Coombs (as Cissie Lupin), Lally Bowers and Diana

King. Written by Michael Ashton and Pam Valentine, it was very much a vehicle for Peggy who dominated the series as the undoubted star. Impatient, intolerant and domineering, the character of Flora Petty was another battleaxe role for which Peggy was ideally suited.

At the time Pam Valentine would say:

We had Peggy Mount and Pat Coombs in mind when we started writing. We would have been very disappointed if we hadn't been able to get them. Fortunately, though, they seemed to take to the idea straight away. We believe that English character actresses are the best in the world but British TV comedy seems to concentrate on male stars. We decided to try and redress the balance.[2]

Pam had never met Pat before the first day of rehearsals. She was immediately impressed:

I thought, 'Oh wow, you're going to be so good in this'; she knew the character and the sort of person she was playing – and she was brilliant. I was knocked sideways by her performance and by her; just the sweetness of her and the funniness of her, the looks across the room when Peggy said or did something a bit naughty... we'd have to look away before we got the giggles, because she was a giggler and she could get the giggles in a show.

During one scene when Peggy had to lean back in a chair and 'fighting hysteria', Patty was helpless and you know when you watch it that she had gone – never to the point of ruining a scene because she had great control, but you could tell that she was struggling. Both were such good actresses with buckets of talent. They could move very easily from comedy to tragedy.[3]

Peggy herself admitted she was pleased to accept the role and that for the previous five years television work had been 'lean' with appearances having been 'few and far between'. Admittedly during those years most of her time had been taken up with work in the theatre; but, ever practical, she would also declare: 'Working in the theatre doesn't do any more than pay the rent.'[4]

Peggy was also thrilled to be working alongside her patient co-star again, saying at the time: 'We make such a natural comedy partnership that it seems incredible that we never even met before *Lollipop*. We have become firm friends since then, and are very happy to be working together again.'[5] Years later Peggy would admit to Pat during a joint television interview, 'I sort of inherited you from Irene Handl.'[6]

The relationship between Mount and Coombs was well remembered by Georgina Moon who played Miss Finch in all four series of the programme. She would recall that Pat was 'lovely and easy-going, and she was very giggly and got quite silly on the set'.[7] The familiarity between the two stars meant that Peggy was more than comfortable in her on-screen physicality with Pat, as Georgina would reveal:

> Pat used to brace herself on the scenes they had together... sometimes with the slapstick Peggy was very full-on and if she had to slightly push Pat or give her a pat on the back she was likely to go flat on her face! They sometimes had rather boisterous scenes together and Peggy would go a bit too far in rehearsals.[8]

Happily the success of the pilot resulted in the series being commissioned, and even bought by overseas television companies. A steady amount of work and recognition for Peggy and her co-stars would subsequently follow. The 'lovely' cast, on the whole, worked very well together, without any of the bitchiness that may have been anticipated by bringing together a mainly female group of actors. Peggy Mount was especially pleased to be working alongside Lally Bowers whose professional career began in 1944 and included numerous successful plays in London's West End. Like Peggy, Lally Bowers had toured the country in her early days in rep and was receiving praise from the critics at the very start of her career. Pam Valentine remembers that Peggy considered her fellow actress to be 'a genius – a superb actress' and constantly pushed for her to be given more lines saying, 'I revere that woman – give her more, give her more.'

By now Peggy's friendship with Pat Coombs was well established. Their time together on the series perhaps consolidated the relationship which continued until Peggy's death. Like most people who ever encountered Pat Coombs, Pam Valentine remembers her as 'one of the loveliest people in the world' but was also conscious that the relationship between Mount and Coombs was 'a friendship that was organised by Peggy... She liked Patty very much to herself. When making the series she'd say, "We'll sit here Patty, or we'll do that Patty," and Patty was so sweet.'

Actor John Standing, a close friend of Peggy's for many years, saw another side to the veteran actress: 'Peggy was always playing gorgons and famous for her mental brutality – rather than her physical brutality – and her vocal brutality, her booming voice and all of that, but she was a darling.'[9]

The slapstick element of the series did not deter Peggy Mount in the least. Despite being in her sixties and heavily overweight during the production of the sitcom, Peggy remained surprisingly agile and, like many larger ladies, incredibly light on her feet. Every element of the series was approached with complete professionalism and according to Pam Valentine 'there was no messing around'. The stark comparison between the tall, stick-thin, lanky frame of Pat

Coombs and the short, stout figure of Peggy Mount inevitably led to the characters being likened to a modern-day female version of Laurel and Hardy. Michael Ashton was quoted as saying, 'They have the timing and understanding of a new Laurel and Hardy,' and Pam Valentine reveals: 'Duncan Wood always used to describe them as a female Laurel and Hardy, although Peggy Mount would have turned into Vesuvius if it was ever said to her.'[10] Ironically Mount did use the analogy, years after the series ended, during a 1992 interview with Terry Wogan.

Aside from their physical differences, which were successfully incorporated into the humour of the series, many facets of the actresses' real-life personalities featured in the scripts; Mount as the blustering, dominant star of the sitcom and Coombs as her timid, easy-going sidekick, often (but not always) reflected their off-screen friendship. As the years passed and Peggy and Pat grew closer, it was often Patty who turned a blind eye to the less engaging elements of Peggy's character. Despite their distinctly different personalities, Pat remained loyal to Peggy, and never more so than during the last several years of their lives.

Although very much the star of the series, Peggy remained, in the words of Pam Valentine, a 'very, very generous artist – she had no objection whatsoever to fellow artists getting the laughs. She would suggest things: "that will be funny, do that"; but if she took against someone that was it. They were out. She was ruthless, and she would say if she didn't want them in the series again.' While Peggy was 'delightful with the other actresses', Valentine admits that veteran Irish actress Peggy Ledger was a prime example of someone who did not escape

Mount's wrath. Ironically Ledger (born in 1900) was the only actress genuinely old enough to be playing a character in a retirement home, but her inability to remember her lines (and occasionally 'fluffing one or two') frustrated the star of the show, who was '100% professional and knew the lines; she worked and worked and worked and she never complained about lines being cut'. As a result of what Peggy Mount considered Peggy Ledger's unprofessionalism, she 'quickly didn't like her'. Mount would stipulate to the writers that Peggy Ledger should have no more than 'five lines per episode' before eventually demanding that Ledger be dropped from the series, saying, 'That's it. I don't want her in it any more.' As Pam Valentine remembers: 'There was no messing about with Peggy Mount and as a result poor old Peggy Ledger got the push.'[11]

Pam would sum up the differences between the two stars of her sitcom in 2020:

> Peggy was such a contrasting character – so difficult, yet so talented and could be, when she wanted, very kind, but Patty was constantly Patty. They had huge respect for each other. Each appreciated the other's value to the show.[12]

In February 1978 Pat was the subject of *This Is Your Life*. She regarded this as another one of the most important events of her career. The biographical television series was hosted by Eamonn Andrews (1955-64 and 1969-87) and involved a special guest being surprised with the 'big red book' of their life. Each subject of the programme would be joined by various family members, friends and colleagues and inevitably surprised at the end of the programme with an extra special guest usually flown in from overseas.

Unbeknown to Pat, in the first weeks of 1978 Thames Television researchers spent several hours with her father and stepmother at their flat in Guilford Court, Walmer, interviewing them about Pat's early life and childhood days. Thomas Coombs would later say, 'It was jolly hard keeping it to ourselves,' and many other family members were also privy to the secret.[13]

On the pretext of filming a short scene in a bingo hall with Peggy Mount and other cast members from *You're Only Young Twice*, Pat was duly surprised (or gobsmacked in her own words) by Eamonn Andrews with the legendary words, 'Pat Coombs – *This Is Your Life.*' Immediately slipping into one of her 'funny voices' she admitted, 'I went to have me picture taken. I'd have gone in a long frock if I'd known!'

In addition to her father, stepmother and brother, Pat was joined by a host of friends and colleagues, and to complete the occasion her sister Pam was flown in from Canada (twelve years after she had emigrated there) as an extra surprise at the end of the show. Pre-recorded messages came from those who were unable to be there in person. Hugh Lloyd would describe Pat as 'one of the finest comedy actresses on the box' and also mentioned her work for the Samaritans, thanking her on the organisation's behalf. Rod Hull and his sidekick Emu would also make an appearance, with Rod saying affectionately, 'We miss you… carry on making us laugh.'

Irene Sutcliffe would recall their time at LAMDA and the Octopus Club, revealing Pat would always bring the grander members of their group 'down to earth' with one of her funny voices and saying: 'Whenever Pat was around there was always laughter… there is more to her than just a funny lady… she has a unique capacity for friendship – she has an incredible ability to assume any accent or dialect at the drop of a hat… ask her a question and the reply might come in Cockney, American, a broad Yorkshire.' Irene was accompanied by Frieda Hodgson, dressed in her trademark manner, who remembered Pat as one of the LAMDA 'family', recalling how she came back to teach and how she was now highly regarded as one of the examining board and a 'critical expert who makes all the candidates absolutely at one with you from the moment go, and I can't tell you how grateful we all are'.

Her childhood friend Sheelagh Hoblyn, to whom Pat was bridesmaid in 1951, also appeared in the programme, accompanied by her son (Pat's namesake godson, Patrick), as did Irene Handl who received rapturous applause as she slipped into her Mrs Purvis character and voice, with the unforgettable catchphrase 'Come to mummy, darlin'… here she comes.' The entire cast of *You're Only Young Twice* was also in the studio, led by Peggy Mount who would describe Pat as 'not only a friend but one of the finest comedy actresses I've ever worked with'.

Dick Emery was another friend who sent a pre-recorded message. Pat's face lit up when she saw him on screen and she immediately addressed him with the words 'Hello Maud'. He went on to say:

> Whenever we've worked together we've had a good time… whenever I think about you I always laugh and it's a wonderful thing to have that laughter between two people, as you and I've got… I want you to know, quite sincerely, that I've always admired you as an actress, bless your heart, and as a great character actress… I only wish I could be there with you to have a couple of drinks and tell you how much I love you.

Another heartfelt pre-recorded tribute was made by Bob Monkhouse (the pair greeted one another with 'Hello Patty'/ 'Hello Bobby'), who rightly said that Pat could play any part he could write: 'We've been together through good times and bad times and loved one another well for a good many years… you bring cheer and happiness to the people working with you… super lady.'

Among the final guests on the show were Pat's *Beggar My Neighbour* co-stars, June Whitfield, Reg Varney and Peter Jones. Pat would repeat her catchphrase in the show, 'My lips are sealed,' for Reg Varney – who responded by giving her an affectionate kiss on the cheek – and Peter Jones would recall Pat's coolness during their times together on the series after her car was stolen, and then found – minus the wheels and engine! June would remember the outrageous earrings Pat wore during the series (and frequently corpsing on set just by looking at Pat) before ending the show with the words:

> Not only are you – in everybody's eyes – the most smashing person to work with, but you are just about the kindest, most warm-hearted person that we could wish to meet and you will do anything to help anybody at any time.

Sadly, the television tribute was the only one Pat received during her lifetime. It is possible, had she lived longer, that her work in radio and television (and her considerable efforts for charity, particularly the Osteoporosis Society) would have been celebrated with some kind of lifetime achievement award or perhaps more formal recognition in the form of an MBE or even OBE. In the 1980s, 1990s and beyond, Pat watched as other contemporaries and former co-stars (including Beryl Reid, June Whitfield, Peggy Mount and Barbara Windsor) received accolades for their years in the business, yet Pat's contribution to the arts and charity went unrecognised.

Although Pat was thrilled with her *This Is Your Life* tribute, two people who were key in her life at that time were noticeably absent: the writers of *You're Only Young Twice*, Michael Ashton and Pam Valentine. In 2017 Pam Valentine revealed: 'Unfortunately for no good reason Peggy took against Michael – she wasn't rude but she ignored him – regardless of the fact that our combined work was keeping her way up there.'

It was actually Pat who revealed that Peggy's dislike of Ashton stemmed from her belief that he was responsible for one of her actor friends being sacked from a theatre company. Pam Valentine remembers the situation with sadness: 'Mike was a very good theatre director and there was an actor in the company who simply wasn't very good and Mike in fact had to sack him. If Michael had been horrible to this man, who she had taken to her bosom, then she decided she wasn't going to like Michael. It was typical Peggy. She was very childish. She was very, very difficult.'[14]

When it came to Pat's *This Is Your Life* episode, such was Peggy's dislike for the series co-writer that she warned producer Graeme Muir, 'If they invite him I won't go.' As a result neither Ashton nor his co-writer attended the occasion, which later caused Pat to question where Pam and Michael both were. Pam would later confirm that Pat was 'heartbroken' by their absence.[15] Likewise Peggy always refused to have a group photograph of the cast and crew because she would not be seen alongside Ashton. Pam believes Peggy's animosity towards Michael had a major impact to the longevity of the series, and even Peggy's television career as a whole:

Silly old sausage! We could have gone on longer if she didn't have this insane dislike of Michael who was the sweetest guy – everybody loved him. I think she built up such a dislike – and thought she would be doing so many more things, but of course she didn't. She didn't take against me – and quite wanted me to be her buddy, but I couldn't cosy up to her and be her buddy – I had to take a pleasant line of always being courteous and friendly but not being girly, girly with her. If she hadn't taken against Michael I think the series would have run longer than it did.

Peggy Mount was fundamentally a kind person but struggled throughout her life to display affection or accept personal praise or thanks in any real way. Professional recognition was always well received, but allowing her steely veneer to slip in private in order to accept affection or thanks was difficult for Peggy. A prime example of this personal trait was recalled by Pam Valentine:

If anybody mentioned they couldn't get hold of something or they were looking for something, nothing was said but the following Sunday at the read-through she would turn up and stuff something in their hands. She heard me say one day, 'Why can't you get a little metal teapot for one person?' and the following Sunday she walked into rehearsal and said 'Teapot' and shoved it in my hands. I tried to say, 'Oh Peggy, that's so thoughtful,' but she just said, 'Oh, doesn't matter'… she was almost embarrassed by her own niceness. She really was her own worst enemy. Her instincts were kind but something in her prevented her from letting her guard down; obviously she had a weird childhood and the difficult relationship with her sister. She never talked about her family at all. She had a very kind, poor, sad, lovely side to her.[16]

One of Peggy's colleagues on the series was Johnnie Wade, whose fifty-year career in entertainment included singing in cabaret and work in films and television. He would play Roger the handyman in all four series of *You're Only Young Twice* and as a result got to know Peggy well. At the time of recording the programme he would say of Peggy and Pat:

> They are kind of mother figures to me. When we are working together in Leeds, I like to go out for a bit of a rave round the clubs. And when we meet up in the morning there is often an inquest: 'Where were you last night, Johnny?' they ask me.[17]

In 2017 he would remember Peggy, who became such a key player in Pat's final years, with frankness:

> Peggy Mount was a very difficult person to understand; if she didn't like you, that was that! She was very generous on the one hand but quite vindictive and spiteful on the other. She would knit various items of clothing for members of the cast – none of which fitted – and poor old Patty Coombs had to model some at the rehearsal rooms through gritted teeth. She would also cook cold-water pastry pies which were inedible; little gifts for the cast at the end of each series were another thoughtful gesture.
>
> I would drive her up to Leeds for the show and she would let me use the car for the weekend and I would drive her home and pick her up the next day, except one day I forgot to pick her up for rehearsal. My God, did the shit hit the fan then; the whole cast waited for the explosion. Graeme Muir was having kittens and was mumbling 'sorry' to everyone. She didn't disappoint; when she arrived she burst through the doors and kicked Patty's handbag the length of the room, glared at me and told Graeme she was not to be spoken to.
>
> The other side to her nature became evident early on; for some reason she took against the writers Pam and Michael (who created the series for her) and refused to talk to them and only took notes from the director, which was ludicrous, but this went on for the whole series. She refused to sit next to Graeme's wife at the cast meals calling her 'That Woman'. She was the star and everyone knew it. God help any of the extras who sat on her chair on set. The cast were great and very patient... let's face it we all needed the work.[18]

Despite Peggy's dominant persona, the series allowed both ladies to shine. In many ways, as one of Pat's obituaries later pointed out, she managed to 'upstage' Peggy Mount 'much to Mount's off-screen amusement. It was something no other actress had ever dared to do.'[19]

During their years working together, Pat and Pam Valentine became good friends. Pam was one of very few people who were privy to Pat's occasional times of depression. She would remember her multi-faceted chum with honesty:

> She was such a darling. There can't be anyone with anything bad to say about her because she so understanding, thoughtful, kind, generous.
>
> She was such a very shy person, self-effacing, it was hard to convince her how talented she was, and she was insecure and this led to times of deep depression caused by loneliness. She adored her family… she obviously loved her nieces very much but she was lonely at times and then she drank a little too much.
>
> She used to ring me when she was very low, and this could be at 1am in the morning, but it didn't matter, I was pleased she felt she could ring. She could be quite bitter in her speech – not about other people but just about not having achieved what she wanted to achieve – to be more than someone else's sidekick, probably. She was always 'number two' but of course she was very funny.
>
> She was a very private lady. Only in depression did she admit and pour out her sadness saying things like, 'I'm alone, I've got no one, no one cares, and I've had a terrible career.' I would reassure her and say, 'You know you're talking cobblers. You're having a down time. You've had a brilliant career and you are dearly loved – come on, come on.'
>
> I think underlying everything there was a sadness that she hadn't married, that she hadn't had children, and that she hadn't perhaps had the career she longed for. But she kept working and not everyone can have their names in lights. It was like the grain of sand inside the oyster that irritates and irritates but you forget that grains of sand turn into pearls.

In many ways she was a strange combination; she knew how good she was, she had huge talent, but so unassuming and self-effacing. Such a lovely dry sense of humour… great on one-liners.

Everybody loved her and you can't say that about many people.[20]

Pam admits that many of the early-morning telephone calls she received from Pat contained 'confidences I could never repeat… sad things she said when she was unhappy', but she was also aware how strong Pat could be for other people. Ever loyal, Pat was an extremely good listener and would never betray the trust of the many friends and colleagues who confided in her over the years.[21]

In times of stress Pat did admit to finding solace in alcohol and cigarettes. When she was controversially dropped from the cast of *EastEnders* (see Chapter 8) she would reveal, 'I did a lot of sitting at home with a glass of wine… I didn't hit the bottle, but I was drinking more than usual and I started smoking more heavily too. I went up from 20 More Specials a day to over 30 and I put on weight.'[22] Over a decade earlier she had hinted at her loneliness in the press saying, 'I do sometimes get fed up with my own company. I'm quite happy to sit down in my flat by myself. Basically I'm a very lazy person.'[23] As well as white wine Pat also had a taste for brandy – which Pam Valentine feels 'really acted as a depressant'.

I remember her coming to my room at the Queen's once – I don't know how it happened – and I had a half bottle of brandy which I travelled with for emergencies and she drank quite a lot of it, which didn't matter; but the next time we met she very discreetly gave me a bag and in it was a half bottle of brandy, and she said, 'I felt so bad about drinking your brandy last week,' and I said, 'You didn't have to do that,' and she said, 'Oh yes I did' – which was so Patty – 'I had to say thank you, I have to replace your brandy.'

Realising that her fondness for alcohol was beginning to become a problem, Pat subsequently sought professional help to curb her drinking habit. In her own matter-of-fact way, and perhaps bearing in mind her brother's premature death, she attended Alcoholics Anonymous. With their help and guidance she was able to cut back on her alcohol consumption. Although she never stopped drinking, and to the end of her days thoroughly enjoyed a glass of wine, she was at least able to stop herself becoming overly reliant on alcohol. Throughout her difficult periods, work undoubtedly provided Pat with a lifeline and she revelled in accepting new offers, saying at the time: 'I'm the last person to grouse and I'm a bit idle so I'll go on as long as people want me to.'[24]

Although *You're Only Young Twice* ran for four series and Pat received praise in the press as 'a comedy actress whose timing is like that of Big Ben',[25] it was not admired by everyone with one critic writing scathingly: 'I sat patiently through *You're Only Young Twice* in which the central "joke" was the effects Epsom salts in the food had upon the old ladies of Paradise Lodge. Thank heavens it was the last in the series. With material like this I find booming Peggy Mount and simpering Pat Coombs insufferable.'[26] In more recent years the series has been released on DVD and repeated on television and remains much loved by Pat's fans and family, including her nephew Simon Brooks who recalls:

One of Aunt Pat's most memorable scenes in *You're Only Young Twice* that still makes me laugh is the episode where Aunt Pat's character is helping Peggy Mount's character in the kitchen. Aunt Pat was told to wash the lettuce and then toss it. When Peggy asked where the lettuce was, Aunt Pat replied that she washed the lettuce with soap and then tossed it... then Aunt Pat looked up – the lettuce was hanging off a ceiling light.[27]

Generally speaking Pat and Peggy's efforts were welcomed and their defining roles have gone down in television history as highlights of both their careers. Pat regarded the production as 'such fun' and almost a decade after the final series thought it would be 'smashing' if the programme was resurrected. It remained one of her personal favourites, and as late as 1999 she still held out hopes that a new series would be made. By this time both Peggy and Pat were in poor health, and in light of this Pat admitted: 'The insurance on us both would go through the ceiling.'[28] Nevertheless it would have been interesting to see how such a series would have been received, although, alas, it never came to fruition.

In the same year as *This Is Your Life* came the death of Pat's stepmother, Phyllis, at the age of eighty. Although she had joined Pat's father for the television special, she was clearly frail, linked by her husband and stepson, Tony, and carrying a walking stick.

In the following year came a much closer blow with the tragic death of Pat's brother at the early age of fifty-three. Tony Coombs died in Sunderland on 26th February 1979, predeceasing his father and leaving behind three children: Nicholas (Nick), Sally and Penny. His marriage to June had ended in divorce but his children had managed to maintain a strong relationship with their extended family, as Penny recollects:

When my parents divorced, 1964ish, my grandparents and aunts still kept in close contact with my mother, sister, brother and me. This was very important to us as we had no other family nearby (albeit a couple of hours' drive away). Pat was very family orientated...

she adored her older brother who took little notice of her and sister Pam. But that was my father for you.[29]

After drifting apart during their childhood it took many years for Pat and her brother to be partly reunited, and even then they were never especially close.

Although Tony did remarry, his second union was short-lived; he was officially separated at the time of his death but never divorced his second wife. He was largely estranged from his children in later years, although he did continue to send Christmas and birthday cards; token gestures largely, his daughter Penny feels, at the behest of Thomas Coombs. A lifetime battle with alcoholism combined with a congenital heart condition totally undermined Tony's health. Not long before his death he casually informed Pat that he no longer needed to take his heart medication. When his weekly Sunday telephone call to his father was missed for two consecutive weeks, Thomas Coombs contacted the local police who broke into Tony's small flat. They found he had been dead for almost a fortnight.

It was a sad demise for Pat's only brother; and a decade after his death she would say, 'When I look back I think the pity is that Tony and I didn't really hit it off. It was only in the latter years of his life that we even got near to becoming friends. It was such a shame.'[30] Privately she considered his death 'at a very early fifty-three' a 'sad tale' which would draw links with the death of his only son just five years later.[31]

Pat's father, meanwhile, lived on into his eighties. Having survived two wives and one child, Thomas Coombs spent the last years of his life living in a Masonic Home in London before his death in Bromley, Kent, on 17th May 1982.[32] Pat remained forever grateful for the love and stability her parents had given her throughout her life and especially during her formative years. Finding herself an 'orphan' in her fifties was a cross she had to bear, but she continued to enjoy a strong relationship with her sister Pam and her extended family which happily grew to include great-nephews and nieces.

In 1981, when Pat was still immensely busy with a variety of projects, including *You're Only Young Twice* and a multitude of commercials and voice-over work, she was commissioned to write her autobiography. An advance was duly paid, but despite the press hailing it as 'destined to be a bestseller' the project never really got off the ground. Pat admitted at the time, 'I'm finding "the book" very hard, and I've still got several thousand words to write.'[33]

In 1999 she would reveal to me:

Am ashamed to tell you (and thought you maybe knew already) I was given a big advance fee way back in '81 for my autobiography… I wrote about a fifth of same and called it 'Getting It Off Pat!' and returned the money… HOW MAD CAN YOU GET?! 'Twas part laziness… but also an emotional sort of hiccup when I came to write about my beloved mum and ditto George (the one I should've married!)… 'Nuff said… folk keep on at me and I know I should do it… but, with failing memory etc, me thinks 'tis too late![34]

Typically, Pat kept the manuscript to what she described as 'the book that never was' until her death.[35] It was seen by her niece, Penny Hey, who remembers it amounted to a very small amount of work, although she did not read it. If the 'manuscript' is still in existence its current whereabouts are sadly unknown.

7

Changing times

'A twinkle in her eye'

BY THE END OF THE 1970s Pat Coombs had well and truly
carved a unique niche for herself within British entertainment.
Whenever a tall, timid, slightly jittering 'foil' was needed by
casting directors she was the obvious choice. In many ways,
with her immense vocal talents and distinctive looks, she was
totally unique and only a couple of actresses spring to mind
who were even slightly in the same mould as Pat – although
neither would achieve her level of professional success.
Previously the character actress Agnes Lauchlan, described in
one obituary as 'immensely tall', 'an English eccentric if ever
there was one' and an 'odd-bod'[1] had appeared on stage and
film (from 1924 and 1937 respectively) playing eccentrics but
never became a household name, despite working on television into her seventies. Likewise another jittering eccentric,

in the form of the distinctive bit-part player Lucy Griffiths (who was candidly described by actress Damaris Hayman as a 'prize parasite'),[2] also played similar characters to those taken on by Pat, but with limited scope.

While her contemporaries often complained about being typecast, Pat was more than happy with her exclusive place within the acting profession. From her earliest days in the business she realised that her role as Nola in *Hello Playmates* had often resulted in her playing dim-witted individuals, and once admitted: 'I've been asked if there is anything of me in the character!' She would later say: 'People always seem to feel sorry for me because I play these soppy, put-upon characters on TV; I think they're quite relieved to find I'm fairly normal, and that I'm not really as daft as some of the characters I play.'[3] On being frequently cast as a 'doormat' Pat remained philosophical, saying in 1989, 'It's sad isn't it? You'd think I'd been dominated somewhere along the line in my life, but I haven't. I'm not unhappy about it, though, because it's given me a great career.'[4] Georgina Moon would compare Pat to another comedy legend: 'She was a bit like John Inman – who wasn't this camp, Mr Humphries/*Are You Being Served?* character – and Pat was not the lovely strange character she was in *You're Only Young Twice...* she was a very bright lady.'[5]

After more than thirty years in the business and with an impressive list of credits to her name, Pat was determined to continue working and would remain busy on television and radio until the very end of her life.

The early 1980s saw Pat appearing in guest roles on television, notably as the 'interfered-with court witness' in Robert Gillespie's series *Keep it in the Family*. Robert would later remember Pat as an 'absolutely wonderful lady' and the episode in which she guest-starred got him the 'biggest laugh – ever!'[6] Radio also continued to provide many opportunities to work with some of the best-known names in the business, including Sheila Hancock in *Thank You Mrs Fothergill* and *Know Your Place*. Although Sheila would admit 'I am afraid I knew Pat very little,' in her eighty-seventh year she penned a unique tribute to her colleague:

> She was a delight to work with. A gentle, attractive woman quite unlike the parts she was often called upon to perform. Like me, she worked with many comics, providing them with the support and perfect timing they required, never seemingly wanting to be in the limelight herself, happy to feed their laughs. She seemed to me a thoroughly nice woman.[7]

Having been thrilled at being the subject of *This Is Your Life* in 1978, Pat was always happy to greet fellow professionals when they were the lucky recipient of the 'big red book'. In 1982 she joined Irene Sutcliffe and over half a dozen other former LAMDA students when Eamonn Andrews surprised the legendary 'blonde bombshell' actress, Diana Dors. By this stage – having been regarded for many years as Britain's answer to Marilyn Monroe – the ever-glamorous Dors had proven her worth as an excellent actress in all areas of the profession as well as becoming a beloved national figure. Pat received rapturous applause as the last of LAMDA's graduates to greet Diana, and there was clearly deep affection between the two ladies who had often seen each other over the decades (featuring together, for example, in a 1976 episode of *Celebrity Squares*). Pat's scrapbook photograph of Diana (minus the caption) had been used in the programme and she would immediately slip into one of her funny voices, saying, ''Ere, Di, do you remember at LAMDA?' to which Diana replied, 'I'll never forget! You were the comedienne and I was the mad girl.' To the delight of the audience Pat went on to say, 'No! No! Listen. I got all them lovely parts – romantic, sexy, you weren't half jealous. But we're still best of mates – right?' A beaming Diana Dors replied, 'Of course!' as the two ladies laughed at their salad days over thirty years earlier. Sadly, despite looking the picture of good health at the time, Diana Dors would die just two years later, on 4th May 1984, at the age of fifty-two.

Scriptwriter Johnny Speight made it known for years that he wanted to team Pat with fellow character star Patricia Hayes in a television series. It was reported in 1976 that the pair were due to film an unnamed pilot in which they played joint owners of the Excelsior Hotel, 'a seedy though splendid-sounding establishment in the South London suburb of Catford'.[8] Both Pat and Patricia Hayes were great admirers of Speight's work and both had guest-starred in his popular series *Till Death Us Do Part* (starring Warren Mitchell).[9] One scene in particular (where the two Pats gossiped away completely ignoring the yells of Alf Garnett who was trapped in a window high above them) had delighted Speight who was quoted as saying, 'It was as a direct result of this scene that I decided to write a series for them. I regard them as an unbeatable team for comedy.'[10]

Talk again turned to uniting the two ladies in another series, titled *Gas Bags*, with Patricia Hayes (as Min) playing a tea lady at the Houses of Parliament, with Pat playing her sidekick, Maggie. Jack Bentley, for the *Sunday Mirror*, wrote that '*Gasbags* will be the most topical comedy ever made. Each show will be shot on one day and broadcast the next.' Johnny Speight added: 'The show will allow me to make ordinary people like Min say what they think of the people who run the country. It will be like Min and Maggie having their own little parliament within Parliament. They can spread all kinds of rumours.'

This particular idea sadly never got off the ground, but Speight never forgot how well the two ladies worked together. Seven years later his dream team were finally given their own series.

The Lady is a Tramp, described as 'eminently worthy of air time', ran for two series between 1983 and 1984. Having won a BAFTA award for her portrayal of a vagrant in *Edna the Inebriate Woman*, Patricia Hayes was perfectly cast as Old Pat, a tramp living rough in a disused wheel-less van, having been removed from a succession of park benches. Pat was cast as her 'steady companion', Lanky Pat.[11]

The series would feature a superb range of guest actors including, amongst many others, Brian Wilde, Bill Treacher (with whom Pat later worked in *EastEnders*), Harry Fowler, Roy Kinnear, Gerald Sim, Kate Williams and even Warren Mitchell. It was well received. Critic Mary Kenny wrote: 'Old Pat and Lanky Pat are cheerfully sharp and comically erudite.' The storylines and dialogue, like many of Speight's other comic creations, were not without controversy and Kenny admitted: 'There will be complaints about this programme for being sexist, ageist and insensitive to the plight of the homeless – but there will be much laughter too.'[12] For their work on *The Lady is a Tramp*, Pat and Patricia Hayes received the Pye Television Award for best comedy actress in 1983.

Pat's mother, Hilda May
(1898-1971), with her parents,
Thomas and Florence Ball.

Pat's paternal grandparents, Thomas
Coombs (Mayor of Camberwell)
and his wife, Fanny.

Pat Coombs (Patricia Doreen Coombs).

Pat Coombs (in white bonnet) with her
mother and elder brother, Tony.

Pat with her maternal grandmother and elder brother.

The Coombs family in the 1930s. Trips to the seaside were a popular activity for the family.

An early studio portrait of Pat. By the age of six she had already decided that she wanted to be an actress.

Pat as a teenager. After leaving school she would initially work as a kindergarten teacher.

Pat's elder brother, Anthony (Tony) Thomas Coombs, during his time in the Royal Navy.

Pat's father, Thomas Coombs (1898-1982), and his second wife, Phyllis.

Pat during her time as a student
at LAMDA, 1945/46.

Pat on stage in Nottingham as Poppy
Dickey in *Rookery Nook*, 1948.

Ever the bridesmaid: Pat at
the wedding of her friends
Graham and Sheelagh Hoblyn,
2nd June 1951.

A unique caricature of Pat drawn by
her close friend and frequent
colleague, Bob Monkhouse.

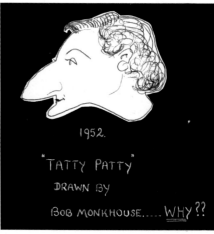

1952.

"TATTY PATTY"

DRAWN BY

BOB MONKHOUSE..... WHY ??

The Isle of Wight was a favourite holiday destination for Pat.

RETURN to FISHBOURNE.
1953.

"OAKDENE AGAIN."

Pat with her mother and younger sister, Pam, in the 1950s.

Pat in her twenties. Tall and slim, she admitted to having the 'pipe cleaner look'.

Pat with her parents and younger sister in the 1950s. The Coombs family remained a tight-knit unit even after Pam's marriage and move to Canada.

Pat in 1953, a few years before she became an established radio star.

(Photo: ANL/Shutterstock)

The cast of *Great Scott, It's Maynard* – Bill Maynard, Shirley Eaton,
Pat Coombs and Terry Scott.

(Photo: Ron Stilling/ANL/Shutterstock)

'The one I should have married.'
George Raistrick in the 1950s.

George Raistrick (in his trademark
fedora hat) in later life. He remained
friends with Pat until his sudden death
in 1995. (Photo: courtesy of Lisa Blunt,
reproduced with permission)

Publicity photographs of Pat during her early career. At the beginning of
the 1960s she came close to quitting the acting profession.

A rare candid photograph showing Pat on location with Tony Hancock. During her fifty-year career she worked with many of Britain's top comedy actors.

'Nola was such a stupid woman!' Pat dressed as her most famous character from the radio series *Hello Playmates*.

Pat as Queen Elizabeth I on television with Henry McGee.

Pat with her friend and frequent colleague, Dick Emery. As well as working together on stage and screen Pat would appear in more than forty episodes of his television series. (Photo: Shutterstock)

Peggy Mount and Pat Coombs in the television series *You're Only Young Twice*. The pair would spend their final years living at Denville Hall, the actors' retirement home. (Photo: ITV/Shutterstock)

A 'neat' Virgo. Pat had a lifelong interest in astrology.

(Photo: Jon Lyons/Shutterstock)

Pat in the 1972 film *Ooh, You Are Awful* (British Lion Films).

Statler meets Coombs. Pat with some of the cast of *The Muppet Show* at the end of the 1970s.

Pat and her younger sister Pam in the 1980s. The two siblings remained close until Pat's death in 2002.

A doting aunt and great aunt. Pat with her niece, Penny Hey and her son Jack, August 1988.

Reunited. Pat and her dear friend Bob Monkhouse joined forces again in 1993 for a new series of *Celebrity Squares*. (Photo: ITV/Shutterstock)

'… the hardest work I have done since twice-weekly rep'. Pat during her time as a cast member of television's *EastEnders* (photographed with June Brown, Sid Owen and Syd Williams).

Pat photographed in 2000. Despite failing health she continued to work and make public appearances until the very end of her life.

(Photo: Alan Davidson/Shutterstock)

Pat at Denville Hall enjoying her favourite 'tipple', with her sister Pam and a feline friend.

'… sunshine and laughter'. Frail but still smiling – Pat at the end of her life, photographed by Lisa Bowerman.

(Photo: courtesy of Lisa Bowerman, reproduced with permission)

Despite the successful pairing of the two 'Pats', their relationship remained purely professional. Pam Valentine was good friends with both ladies and kept in contact with Hayes until the end of her life (even after she had moved into a nursing home after breaking her hip). She confirms their differences:

Pat [Coombs] was very conscious that work used to go to Pat Hayes – she even got a script with Pat Hayes' name written on, then crossed out – but they were very different people, very dissimilar in their real-life personalities.[13]

Although her work as 'Lanky Pat' generally brought great praise, not all critics were favourable to Pat's talents or persona. Stafford Hildred regarded her as a 'pain', writing in 1984:

I feel the same way about Pat Coombs that lamp-posts feel about dogs. Her sketches with Marti Caine were one of TV's all-time lows. Whatever part she plays, prissy Pat seems exactly the same – inane and insipid.[14]

It says much for Pat's lack of vanity that she duly preserved this scathing attack in her personal scrapbook. The criticism perhaps also showed the sea change that was sweeping British television and in particular British comedy at the time. Pat was well aware of the changes. The rise of alternative comedians such as Rik Mayall, Alexei Sayle, Adrian Edmondson, Dawn French and Jennifer Saunders meant that the kind of genteel sitcoms with which Pat had become synonymous were suddenly out of vogue. As early as 1981 Pat was quoted as saying she didn't particularly like 'black comedy' but was well aware of its increasing popularity. The lack of female comedians was also at the forefront of Pat's mind and she said at the time: 'I can only think of Marti Caine and she is doing a difficult job extremely well.'[15]

Although Pat felt there would always be a need for women in comedy, and therefore never anticipated that she would ever need to retire, her work in television comedy notably decreased after her role in *The Lady is a Tramp*. Thereafter she was largely relegated to guest appearances – rather than starring roles – in a number of sitcoms.

Several years after the final series of *You're Only Young Twice*, Pat reunited with Peggy Mount (and their *Lollipop* co-star Hugh Lloyd) on television in the one-off Channel 4 production, *It's Never Too Late*. Playing pensioner sisters at a local bowls club, they were also joined by veteran actor Harold Goodwin. Written by actor and director Ian Masters, who had previously worked with Peggy Mount on stage, the piece was a gentle four-hander but was not picked up for a series. On the set of the pilot Ian Masters observed that 'everybody liked Pat – she was so nice'. He would also remember her interest in astrology and her prediction that the pilot they were working on would not develop into a success:

> She was quite psychic and delved into something or other and said, 'Do you want to know, because I think I can tell you whether this is going to go ahead or not?' And she said, 'Something has come up and I'm afraid it's not going to be a success.' She definitely had the gift.

Ian would remember Pat with affection:

> She was such a lovely, lovely lady, quite intense in some ways and certainly an intelligent woman, definitely, the complete opposite to what she often portrayed. From what I could see she got on very well with Peggy Mount and they'd done quite a lot together already. Hugh Lloyd didn't have a happy time on the pilot with Peggy Mount; he'd done nothing to her, bless him, but she used to get a funny bee in her bonnet about people... I suppose if you worked with her for a while it broke. She was a bit funny with me when we first met on *The Mating*

Game and then gradually she warmed and was fine. Pat and Hugh
got on really well and Hugh went to Pat all the time – for comfort! [16]

It's Never Too Late proved to be significant since it would
be the last occasion on which Pat and Peggy would act together
on television, although they were later reunited in television
interviews to the delight of their many fans.

In the same year Pat also took part in a gala special of music,
poetry and entertainment at the Theatre Royal, Brighton, to
raise funds for Ethiopian famine relief, joining a staggering
array of well-known names including Keith Barron, Suzanne
Danielle, Frank Finlay, Irene Handl, Patricia Hayes, Patricia
Hodge, Gloria Hunniford, Julia McKenzie, Patrick Mower,
Una Stubbs and Timothy West. As ever she was only too
happy to help yet another good cause.

Despite the changes in television comedy around this time,
many of the old guard were not forgotten and indeed some
were even celebrated, not least the former *Carry On* film star,
Kenneth Williams. While Kenneth's career as a film actor had
ended with the embarrassingly awful *Carry On Emmannuelle*
in 1978, he had managed to maintain a successful career on
television and radio and in voice-over work. As a natural rac-
onteur he was a popular guest on chat shows such as *Parkinson*
and *Wogan* where he proved to be lively, unpredictable and
highly amusing. By the end of his life he jokingly revelled in
his 'cult' status, and both his looks and voice were instantly
recognisable to generations of television viewers.

In a number of ways Pat's life and career mirrored that of
Kenneth Williams. They were both Cockneys, born within
months of each other in 1926; they both became well-known
household names having enjoyed successful careers on radio,

film and television; both largely avoided theatre work once they had become established actors; and both lived alone. In their latter years Pat and Kenneth earned a great deal of their incomes through commercials and voice-over work and on a couple of occasions they even worked together in this medium. Unlike Williams, however, Pat was not an extrovert and had no interest in being feted as an 'iconic' figure. In later years she watched from the sidelines as contemporaries saw a resurgence of their public popularity, particularly in the case of Dame June Whitfield who in the 1990s finally became a star in her own right, familiar to a new generation via her role as Mother in *Absolutely Fabulous*. Despite being undoubtedly loved by the general public, Pat would remain the eternal stooge – a foil or sidekick for seemingly more dominant actors – yet without her support their success and stardom would not have been possible. Having never particularly desired 'star' status, Pat continued to be happy with her lot. Although the days of sketch shows such as *The Dick Emery Show* were now gone, she was able to adapt to the considerable changes in television comedy and moved from 'foil' to character actress. Radio and voice-over work also continued to keep her busy – and would do so until the end.

The death of Dick Emery at the age of sixty-seven in January 1983 was a sad blow for Pat. Emery was one of her oldest friends and they had remained in contact, professionally and privately, since first working together in the 1950s. A host of sordid newspaper headlines appeared following Emery's demise, as ex-lovers gave lurid details about his bedroom antics under headlines which included 'Sex Addict Emery Was A Flop', 'Even My Pink Undies Didn't Turn Him On'[17] and

'Dick Emery's Secret Love Games'.[18] A High Court battle over his will also brought Dick's private life into the public domain. Although Pat preserved some newspaper cuttings detailing such stories, she remained tight-lipped on her friendship with the comedy legend.

*

Amidst the professional success and spate of work Pat enjoyed in the 1980s came personal tragedy with the death of her eldest nephew, Nicholas (Nick) Coombs.

Having been the first-born grandchild of Pat's parents, Nick was always doted upon. Sadly by the time he reached his teenage years he had developed grand mal epilepsy which impacted upon both his physical and mental health. His relationship with his father, Pat's brother Tony, was a difficult one. Tony was not a tolerant man, and following his divorce in the mid 1960s he became an increasingly distant figure to his three children.

Penny Hey would remember her brother, Pat's beloved nephew, and his relationship with their aunt, in 2020:

> They were very close; he used to take me to see her shows being filmed at White City… I think I must have been pretty young, say around twelve; *Beggar My Neighbour* rings a bell. I have a feeling I was under age.
>
> My brother was the oldest of us all and therefore had a special place with Pat, Pam and my grandparents.
>
> Sadly, he suffered mental health problems as he moved into his teenage years and when my father left. He was quite a worry to the family but Pat was always there for him. Pat and I would talk on the phone late into the night worrying about him.[19]

By 1970 Nick had moved to New South Wales, Australia, to live with an aunt in Wollongong. Tall and sporty, he was especially adept at cricket and was selected to try out for the Sussex Cricket Team's First XI. Despite having worked as a statistician for British Airways, his health problems made it increasingly difficult for him to hold down a job. Within a couple of years of moving to Australia he suffered life-changing injuries after being run over by a car; according to one press report 'his feet were broken and never healed. He developed schizophrenia and spent four years in a psychiatric hospital.'[20] After his release from hospital Nick lived around King's Cross in Sydney where he was befriended by local clergymen and workers at the Wayside Chapel. He began writing poetry, earning him the nickname among locals of 'The Poet', and was a familiar figure in cafes and arcades.

Tragically Nick was recognised by one of the Chapel workers, quite by accident, lying in a hospital bed in a coma. He had been discovered by police 'lying unconscious in a back lane with a big lump on the back of his head'. It was later revealed that Nick had a fractured skull and had suffered severe brain damage. One source was quoted as saying, 'No one knows how it got there. Whether he was bashed, run over or just fell, remains a mystery. Nobody will ever know.'[21] It is possible that due to the increasingly violent nature of his epileptic fits Nick could have hit his head on a gutter during a seizure. Whatever the case, the reason behind his injuries remained a mystery.

Reverend Ted Noffs, director of the Wayside Chapel, said of Nick at the time:

He was a sick, sad and lonely man who believed he was born to write. But he wasn't taking care of himself and often forgot to take his medicine. Even when he found it hard to keep in touch with reality he kept on writing… much of it was deranged rubbish, but some of it was extraordinary. [22]

Nick's mother, stepfather and sister Penny flew out to Sydney to be with him and made strenuous efforts to have him flown home to England, sadly without success. Almost forty years after the event, Penny would remember how they struggled to get flights to Sydney and also how Nick's doctors were reluctant to have him moved because of the extent of his injuries.

After spending six months in a coma, Nick Coombs died peacefully in early 1984. Above his hospital bed were words he had written shortly before his injury:

It's the best months
God does try
And the only time
That heaven does bring
death and everything… [23]

Heartbreakingly Pat would later write, 'I shall never forgive myself for not flying over… too cowardly. He was a smashing lad and we knew him so well in his early years.' [24]

*

In the latter half of the 1980s, children's television provided a lifeline to many veteran performers including Pat. She positively revelled in the light-hearted nature of such work, and in many ways it harked back to the sketch show material she had performed in during the previous decade. Pat would be reunited with Rod Hull on television in *Emu's Pink Windmill* in 1986 as a last-minute replacement for his infamous green-faced witch, Grotbags (Pat played Witch Curdle, a 'proxy' witch who struggled to be bad, when Carol Lee Scott was unavailable), and would return to the series for three episodes in the following year as Lady Petunia, with her former stage colleague Susan Maughan. She would also make two guest appearances in *Super Gran*, the series starring Gudrun Ure as a Scottish grandmother with superhuman powers, based upon Forrest Wilson's books. Despite a small budget and endearingly awful scripts, *Super Gran* would attract a staggering number of some of Britain's best-known veteran actors including Roy Kinnear, Charles Hawtrey, Murray Melvin, Leslie Phillips, Patsy Rowlands, Joan Sims, Patrick Troughton and Barbara Windsor. Another light-hearted project saw Pat working alongside 'Nookie Bear' ventriloquist Roger de Courcey and pupils from Nelson First School in Norwich on a pop video to help make Britain's roads safer for children.[25]

By far Pat's best-known and best-remembered work in children's television came with her role as the 'Little Dressmaker' in thirty episodes of *Ragdolly Anna* (1982 and 1985-87) for Yorkshire Television. She would also narrate the series and provide additional voices in the programme, including those of Ragdolly Anna and the White Cat, who had difficulty pronouncing his r's. The series was based upon a series of books written by Jean Kenward, who never actually met Pat in person but discussed her frequently with the producers of the series.

The Little Dressmaker was charmingly described in the original story, and in some ways her life mirrored that of the actress who subsequently played her:

On the fifth floor of a block of flats in the middle of a certain city there lived a Little Dressmaker. Having neither husband nor children, she made a home for herself with a cat, a geranium, and a large dining-room table with curly legs. On the table sat a sewing machine, and in a corner of the room facing the light stood a tailor's Dummy.[26]

Jean Kenward considers that Yorkshire Television did an 'excellent job' of adapting her 'very simple' fictional character for the small screen and admits: 'I still have people – aged about forty – telling me they were brought up on *Ragdolly Anna*. It's quite astonishing really.'

Jean began writing at the age of eight and went on to write for BBC Schools radio. She continues to pen poetry anthologies to this day, and just months before her 100th birthday she would remember her famous creation:

I particularly didn't want her [Ragdolly Anna] to be a stupid-looking doll – I wanted her to be eager and intelligent, like the child she was written for. The other characters came out well, including the White Cat… one of my children was very intellectual so I modelled the White Cat on him – he didn't really know I was doing it! The Dressmaker was very poor so everything had to be homemade. That was very important.

Ragdolly Anna was produced by Anne Wood, who went on to co-create *Rosie and Jim*, *Tots TV* and most famously *Teletubbies*. For Anne, when it came to casting the role of the Dressmaker, Pat was an instant choice. In 2019 she would recall their professional association and friendship:

I loved Patty – she was gorgeous. I had always admired her work – she'd done radio and Dickens and Little Nell and was brilliant and I needed someone of experience.

We used to laugh about *Ragdolly Anna* because the stories were about a 'little' dressmaker and there was no way Pat was little, she was quite tall, but you could rely on her every time to get the tone of it just right... I didn't want anyone to be sickly sweet, she was absolutely on the button every time. She used to talk to this doll and we used to fall about laughing – we had a lot of laughs, she and I, and there was one time we nearly set the studio on fire because there was supposed to be a birthday cake and we brought in the cake with candles on it and the whole thing self-combusted. The special effects were very basic and would test anybody but she played it perfectly straight.

They were charming stories and she maintained that charm because she did have charm, Patty, she had immense charm and was a really good listener. She smoked too much of course which was her demise, poor woman, but she always had a twinkle in her eye and that is what I will always remember Pat for – and a dry sense of humour.

She took to this doll programme absolutely and after that I used her whenever I could for voice-over, when I was at TV-am and then independent production; I used her in *Playbox* – a series long forgotten – with Keith Chegwin.

Pat enjoyed innocent fun – and that's what we do at Ragdoll and there's an innocence to Jean's stories that belongs to a '*Listen With Mother* age', a different era now... there's still a need for it – but you have to wrap it up differently...

Ragdolly Anna always has a warm place in my heart... it was Patty and the charm of the thing and we just pulled it off and really and truly with the minimum of special effects... if you look at it now, you'd never get away with it but it worked at the time really well. Everybody loved it.

Swansea-born actress Caroline Berry's petite stature allowed her to play the doll's action sequences during the later episodes of the series, having taken over from Michelle Davidson. Caroline was just twenty-six years old in 1987 when she donned Ragdolly Anna's costume, and although she was neither seen nor heard in her first television part she was 'thrilled' to 'scoop' the role.[27] Over thirty years later she would recall:

There'd been another Ragdolly Anna before me but she was replaced and so I got the job. I was working in Harrogate at the time and doing rep so was doing two jobs at the same time! We filmed at the studios in Leeds and on location – Pat was lovely to me and a real 'lady'. We stayed in touch for years afterwards. She was a great comedy actress, very underrated I think.[28]

The actual technical process of filming *Ragdolly Anna* was something new to Pat. It involved sometimes working alongside the actual prop doll while other scenes involved using a glove-puppet doll or a live actor inside a costume of the doll in order to film her moving, as Caroline explains:

Well from what I remember (and it was a very long time ago!) Patty would talk to the inanimate doll and then I would do all the movement… skipping, holding an umbrella, etc. I did my stuff in the studio on a blue background I think (green screen now). I remember us being on location once at a fairground and there were those chairoplanes. I think Pat must have gone on one with Ragdolly Anna.[29]

Ragdolly Anna was described as 'a very special doll, even though she's only made from a morsel of this and a tatter of that'.[30] Despite her simplicity she endeared herself to various ages. Pat's time on the programme brought her a new generation of fans, even within her own family. Over thirty years after the series ended, her great-niece, Georgia (Georgie) Ross, still has in her possession a prop which remains a treasured possession: 'Auntie Pat gave me the doll from *Ragdolly Anna*, complete with her wardrobe, which I still have to this day.'[31] There were of course several versions of the famous creation; the original still resides with Jean Kenward who admits: 'People who were brought up on the series still come to see her!'[32]

The programme's catchy theme tune is also well remembered to this day, and singer Allan Taylor clearly recalls being assigned to the project:

> Keith Morgan (Head of Music at Yorkshire Television, which commissioned the project) asked me to write a song for the series... However Keith said the producer insisted that her lyrics should be used. This took a bit of arranging as her lyrics didn't have any rhythmic metre. I wrote and arranged the music in a ragtime style. We recorded the piece at YTV studios in Leeds.[33]

Around the same time as the second series of *Ragdolly Anna*, and well over a decade after her last appearance in a period drama, Pat was cast in a small role as Mrs Guppy in one episode of the all-star, award-winning BBC miniseries *Bleak House*, starring Dame Diana Rigg and Denholm Elliott. Despite a number of similar productions which would follow over the next decade in which she could have appeared, it would be Pat's final foray into a costume drama. She seemed to take more pleasure from featuring in light-hearted productions, especially in further children's television series, where her voice once again proved to be her finest asset.

In 1987 Pat was clearly elated to be among a staggering array of stars on *Wogan's Radio Fun*. The two-part special celebrated the 'Golden Years' of radio comedy. It provided a unique opportunity to bring together some of the best-known names of the boom years of radio including, amongst others, Harold Berens, Bernard Braden and his wife Barbara Kelly, Maurice Denham, Jimmy Edwards, Cyril Fletcher, Deryck Guyler, Pearl Hackney, Patricia Hayes, Leslie Phillips, Cardew Robinson and Molly Weir. To the absolute delight of fans Pat joined Irene Handl and Bob Monkhouse on the programme, resurrecting her character of Nola from *Hello Playmates*. Monkhouse regarded Mrs Purvis and Nola as 'the most delightful characters' in the series' seven-year run. Despite failing health (she was suffering from metastasised breast cancer), Irene Handl remained a working actress to the end of her long life. Her final television appearances were on a couple of episodes of Terry Wogan's programme, where she thrilled audiences despite her obvious frailty. When Irene (dressed as Mrs Purvis) introduced Nola, her 'unspoilt baby Venus' Pat emerged also dressed in character as her famous radio persona. The reunion was hilarious as Mrs Purvis beckoned her daughter, 'You come out here to Mummy, darlin',' and then described her as 'just one long U-turn on the great motorway of life'. In her appearance with Irene and Bob, it was clear that Pat was struggling not to 'corpse' as she listened to Irene's superb and seemingly effortless comic timing. Although brief, the reunion was unforgettable.

Pat and Irene Handl had remained in close contact since the 1950s. Anne Wood remembers the pair were 'big friends and Patty did a wonderful impersonation ("I know, Pattyyy") of Irene – she was a really good mimic'.[34] The two ladies had many similarities; both well known for slipping into their 'silly' voices and for their passionate love of animals – in Irene's case her succession of pet chihuahuas, who were 'notorious for nipping people'.[35] Neither of the ladies ever married or had children and both enjoyed living simple lives out of the public eye. Irene was undoubtedly a lovable eccentric. She remained active and unconventional into her eighties, as remembered by her friend Maurice Leonard:

She was a regular sight in the Notting Hill area, attending the all-night screenings of horror films at the local cinema, which she adored, happily plodding along the streets in the dead of night. At the height of the *E.T.* hype, though, she announced she was not impressed. 'I can't get excited about a vacuum attachment.' [36]

Since their early radio days in the 1950s the two ladies had of course worked together on a number of occasions and it was fitting that they would be immortalised on the small screen just before Irene's death.

When their appearance together was screened on 28th December it turned out to be a posthumous one for Irene Handl who had died peacefully in her sleep at home on 27th November 1987. The passing of one of Pat's oldest and dearest chums was a blow from which she never fully recovered. Pat, along with many other friends and colleagues including Molly Weir, attended Irene's funeral at Golders Green Crematorium on 8th December 1987. Songs by Handl's favourite singers including Elvis Presley and Edith Piaf were played at the event; and, it was reported, 'Her much loved chihuahua dog Rosa was brought along shivering to the chilly but moving ceremony by Irene's agent, Peter Graham.' [37]

Pat would remember Irene always with immense affection, writing in 1999: 'It was a great loss for me and millions when she died peacefully in 1987 at the age of eighty-five.' [38]

8
EastEnders

'the hardest work I have done since twice-weekly rep'

THROUGHOUT HER LIFE PAT FREQUENTLY admitted that she would have made a good secretary – and indeed she would, being naturally bright, methodical, neat and organised. Her lack of ambition also prompted her to reveal in 1989 another, less conventional, career choice: 'As a child, I used to love watching them in Kennedy's [at the Old Kent Road, London] form half a pound of butter – before it came pre-packed. For a long time all I wanted to do was pat butter around.'[1] Despite openly admitting to not being 'ambitious', by the time she reached her sixties Pat had been an actress for forty years. She had become a star on radio and television – an instantly recognisable face and voice – and was now financially secure.

Despite the not inconsiderable wealth that decades of success had brought her, Pat remained instinctively frugal.

Having been brought up during the Great Depression and then surviving the rationing of World War II, her 'careful ways' remained one of her key traits. She had various ways of saving money: envelopes, for example, would often be recycled and postage stamps that failed to be franked would be carefully removed from envelopes and reused or sent back to the recipient (I for one received many 'untouched' stamps back from Pat). Pat rarely bought clothes, instead preferring to buy quality garments that would last and not go out of fashion. She did not mind being seen in the same blouse or dress on numerous social occasions and she wore the same jewellery for most of her adult life – a large green chrysoprase ring, her old engagement ring and later her mother's wedding ring. Occasional clip-on earrings completed her look when she was making a public appearance, including a distinctive pair of theatre masks – but they were all presents which other people had bought for her.

In the 1970s, with her earnings and bank balance increasing rapidly, her accountant advised that she needed to 'get rid of' some of her capital and suggested she invest in property. Her niece, Penny Hey, remembers that Pat (obviously not realising the extent of her wealth) decided to buy a caravan! It was some-what typical of her naivety when it came to financial matters. The caravan alas was never really used by Pat, but instead gave her extended family the opportunity of camping breaks at Hayling Island, as her nephew Simon Brooks remembers:

> As a family, mother would take us for a small week or two trip to Hayling Island. Aunt Pat would often join us for a day or weekend. Relaxing on the beach, visiting family nearby, and connecting with all of us was one of her happy pastimes.[2]

Following on from her success in *Ragdolly Anna*, in 1988 Pat was cast as Miss Flavia Jelley in *Mr Majeika*, a children's series which saw the welcome return to television of Scottish comedy actor Stanley Baxter. Around this time she also changed her agent, having been under the wing of Richard Stone for many years. For the remainder of her career she was represented by Barry Burnett who felt that she came to him because at the time he 'looked after' Gretchen Franklin and Anna Wing, two of the stars of television's *EastEnders*, and Barry remembers that Pat 'always wanted to go into *EastEnders*'. Pat's friend Peggy Mount (who remained with the Richard Stone partnership until her death) meanwhile said at the time, 'Oh, everyone's going to Barry Burnett, he's the flavour of the month,' much to Barry's amusement.[3]

Although Barry admits he didn't get to know Pat especially well and considers that she was 'a bit of a loner', he recalls his former client with affection, saying in 2019:

> We had a very nice relationship and she got into *EastEnders*, which she loved doing. I think it was one of the highlights of her career. She was a very nice, warm, generous lady, great fun to be with and everybody loved working with her… she was a good person to work with… never gave any trouble and always delivered the goods.[4]

Garry Bushell congratulated the BBC for their decision to cast Pat as Marge Green in *EastEnders*, writing, 'It's nice to see someone of her calibre on the box, however lousy the vehicle.'[5] The addition of one of Britain's top comedy actresses was seen as a direct need to 'inject Cockney cheer' into the programme, which was frequently criticised for being overly 'boring and depressing'. Pat was quoted as saying, 'If they want a funny Cockney lady who is prepared to have the mickey taken, they call me. I'm delighted to be in *EastEnders*. It's a programme I have always admired.' An *EastEnders* spokeswoman added, 'Pat will be known to millions of viewers from her many comedy roles. We are delighted such a fine actress is joining the cast.'

Ironically Pat revealed that the character of spinster 'Brown Owl' Marge Green reminded her of childhood days when, as a ten-year-old, she had briefly joined the Girls' Life Brigade in East Dulwich, mainly because she was 'desperate to wear the uniform' which alas never actually happened.[6]

Pat was overjoyed to appear in the popular soap opera saying, 'I got goosebumps when I got the offer. I had the same old thrill as I did when I made my first radio broadcast 40 years ago. It's been my dream to appear in *EastEnders* ever since I switched on the first episode. I'm a real Cockney, born within the sound of Bow Bells.'[7]

Initially Pat had assumed her role in the soap would be a 'one-off' appearance so she was thrilled to be offered a three-month contract, even though it meant losing the deposit on a planned holiday to the Canary Islands.

Although excited by her latest assignment, Pat was also initially very nervous about working on the series, despite having previously worked with some cast members (namely Wendy Richard and Bill Treacher, with whom she was friends). 'It was a bit scary,' she would say at the time, 'like going to a new school when you're a kid. I was so excited on my first day… to go out on that lot and see Albert Square, which I'd only seen as a viewer, was great.'[8]

Her fears had obviously been shared with Barbara Knox, famous for her long-running role as Rita in *Coronation Street*, who wrote:

Darlin Pat,

Thank you for your lovely note. Aren't we crackers? Why are we in show-biz? Two nervous wrecks! But we still manage to have a laugh.

Wonderful to see you. You looked marvellous. I'm dreading my show going out! And don't forget I got TWO chances to make a fool of myself. Lord knows what I did on the panel!!! I'll never work again.

Now you listen lovely lady – *EastEnders* needs YOU. You will be marvellous. You always are. I'll be watching. Very good luck. You've nowt to worry about.

Lots of love as always,
Barbara [9]

Far different from her other television work, Pat admitted: '*EastEnders* is the nearest thing to instant acting that I've done. I'm used to working instinctively because you do in the sort of comedy I've done for years. I found it great training for the rehearse-record pace of *EastEnders*. The kids do it brilliantly but it's we older ones who have to do second takes.' [10] The pace of the work was gruelling and being involved in up to six different episodes in one week resulted in her labelling *EastEnders* 'the hardest work I have done since twice-weekly rep'. [11]

The character of Marge Green was a shy, timid lady whose life was devoted to looking after her invalid 93-year-old mother. Pat was aware the character was very much a 'typical Coombs' role, saying at the time:

Yes, another doormat like most of the characters I've played. It's a corner of the market I've been lucky enough to call my own. People think 'that poor old thing again'. But it's been kind to me so I don't knock it. [12]

Nevertheless she played the role with unbelievable pathos, giving some of the most touching performances of her entire career during her short stint with the series, especially when Marge's mother died. Despite this, once again Pat reiterated that she did not hanker after serious dramatic parts:

> I've never longed to play Saint Joan. No Shakespeare for me, thank you very much. I just stick to what I know best and, in a sense, what the public likes.[13]

The character of Marge Green was well received by both the viewers and critics alike with the *Daily Mirror* writing of the character, 'Pat Coombs plays her marvellously as about the only character worth watching.'[14]

In the midst of her joy at joining the cast of *EastEnders* Pat suffered a burglary at her Middlesex flat. A teenage boy was later arrested for the crime, during which he stole more than £2,500 of goods to pay for drugs. Pat later described the crime as 'so weird', not least because the criminal carefully placed a porcelain pig on her pile of fan mail – leaving a clear message that he was aware he was in the home of a famous actress. Although the incident naturally left Pat feeling 'weak, violated and vulnerable' she refused to move from her beloved flat and indeed would remain there for another ten years.

While Pat's character in the soap was generally regarded as 'comic relief', one storyline revolving around Marge Green and her Brownies group caused controversy and resulted in *EastEnders* receiving a 'public dressing down for portraying Brownies as lager-swilling shoplifters'.[15] Pat admitted, 'I think it went a step too far. I am sure the Brownies don't go swilling lager and taking boyfriends on summer camps. But I don't think it was ever meant to be criticism – it all got taken too seriously!'[16]

During her time working in *EastEnders* Pat gamely took part in a Children in Need special where the cast of the soap appeared in a parody of the American series, *Dynasty*. With Bill Treacher (Arthur Fowler) playing Blake Carrington and June Brown (Dot Cotton) playing Alexis Colby, various other cast members were suitably transformed, including Pam St Clement (Pat Butcher) playing Krystle, Letitia Dean (Sharon) playing Sammy Jo and Gillian Taylforth (Kathy Beale) playing Monica. Pat meanwhile, with her arm in a sling, was almost unrecognisable in her dramatic makeover as the character of Sable (played by glamorous leading lady Stephanie Beacham in the original series). The need for a sling was the result of a 'small' fall in which Pat had broken her wrist; a precursor to more serious health problems which would follow later in the decade.

The role of Marge Green brought Pat back into the public domain – and the viewing public's eye – in a massive way. She would receive many notes of congratulation from friends and peers, including more words of support from Barbara Knox who wrote in Pat's Christmas card: 'See you have been busy. And a delight too. Long may you reign. Often think of those crazy days with Sir Ken!! Lots of love, Keep up the good work.'[17]

While Pat was determined not to retire and continued to accept offers of work until the very end of her life, some of her contemporaries were happily enjoying semi-retirement, not least Larry Grayson from whom Pat received a charming typed letter from 'Cascade', his home in Harcourt Gardens, Nuneaton. His voice and every inflection can almost be heard and it is recorded here in full:

Dear Patty,

Looked in last night – thought you were great and a nice bit to do and very funny, you look super, haven't changed hardly since we first met in the good old days up at Elstree and the Beeb, we always had lots of laughs.

Cannot see myself doing more TV, had an offer for a new series called 'Larry Grayson's Filmarama' but the thought of doing four at a time put me off, it was for Thames but think it would end up going out on 'Sky' and it's too soon for that. It was a movie quiz game and I'm sure I would have loved doing it but I gave it a lot of thought and came up with the not now at this time of life, after 51 years trekking up and down the land many times… TV, Theatres, Concerts, etc, would now like to do what I want, when I want and go where I like, silly really me being 39.

We will keep in touch,

Shall keep watch,

Love

Larry

When Pat's contract to appear in *EastEnders* was not renewed she was devastated. Shortly before Christmas 1989, along with eight others in the show, she was dropped from the series in what was subsequently labelled 'The Albert Square Massacre' and 'a panic clear-out, sparked off by falling ratings'. Initially Pat had not realised that she was effectively being sacked from the popular soap and sadly admitted when she did comprehend the fate of her character 'there was a lump in my throat. You see I'd expected it after the first three months, but not six.'

A typed letter to Pat from Michael Ferguson expressed his regret at losing the popular character of Marge Green:

Dear Pat,

You already know, but I thought I'd just put down on paper how much I've enjoyed your performance as Marge on *EastEnders*, which I believe you played with great skill and sensitivity.

I really am sorry that we're losing the character, but I'm sure you understand that the programme must constantly be changing if it is to remain vigorous and healthy.

I very much hope we may have an opportunity of working together again sometime.

Yours sincerely,

Michael Ferguson,

Executive Producer[18]

For the first time in her career Pat raged against the BBC. She was quoted as saying, 'The silly fools have got it all wrong again. They are hopelessly out of touch. I've found an enormous difference between working for them now and working for them 42 years ago when I first came into the business. Then there was this great friendliness, this sense of togetherness.'[19] She went on to label the corporation 'soulless' and blamed the cast cull partly on the new producer, Mike Ferguson, who within six weeks of being appointed had sacked a total of nine actors – eight of whom had been hired by his predecessor, Mike Gibbon.

Pat's rant at the 'faceless' corporation did not go unnoticed. One journalist labelled her 'petulant', saying, 'She has been around TV a long time and should bow out gracefully, instead of squawking like some starry-eyed beginner finding out for the first time how tough showbiz can be.'[20] Pat herself was well aware of how controversial, unprecedented and out of character her outburst was, saying: 'It sounds awful doesn't it? Sensitive and childish and silly after all my years in the business. But I was heartbroken.'[21]

A campaign quickly began, petitioning to bring back Pat's character, led by Claire Rayner's son, journalist Jay Rayner. Within hours of the news being announced Pat's friends and colleagues 'rallied round', headed by Bob Monkhouse and Larry Grayson as Pat revealed:

> Bob and Larry were wonderful. Bob wanted to phone *The Sun* straight away, but I asked him to wait. I had Bob's wife Jackie on the phone after the Clacton episode where Marge learned that her mum was dead and her gentleman friend has gone from her life. She said she cried her eyes out. And dear Larry was hilarious. 'Never,' he said in that great voice of his, 'Oh no, never!' [22]

A direct letter of support came from *EastEnders* star Michelle Collins (famous for her portrayal as Cindy Beale) saying that Pat was 'too good' to stay in Albert Square.

Indeed support for Pat came from all areas of the profession. Garry Bushell wrote: 'The Marge Must Stay campaign starts here!' [23] while weather presenter and television personality Wincey Willis sent letters praising Pat on her performance, saying in one 'how nice it was' to see Pat in the soap opera and, 'I always thought you have been greatly under used in the last few years. Talent will out, you deserve it.' [24] Pat as ever was humbled and surprised by the praise, writing on the back of the letter to her niece Penny: 'Isn't this really nice?'

Despite her heartbreak Pat was not bitter about the decision but felt consultants failed to respond to the wants and needs of the viewers. Her final stand came when writers suggested 'marrying off' Marge Green. Feeling this went against the very nature of the character, Pat dug in her heels saying, 'I went to Colin Brake, the writer, and said I'd rather not do that idea because it doesn't ring true and he respected my opinion. I didn't speak to the producer about it – I didn't want to.' [25]

Inevitably, following her enforced departure from *EastEnders* and very public criticism of the BBC, Pat wondered what was next in her career. While initially there may have been a slight hope that Marge Green could have returned to Albert Square for occasional guest appearances, Pat's media outburst surely scuppered any chances of that happening. She was now in her mid sixties, past retirement age for women at the time, and had been a professional actress for forty years, yet longevity in the business was no guarantee of work. Garry Bushell, after watching Peggy Mount's striking – yet brief – guest appearance as a Mother Superior in an episode of television's *Morse*, bemoaned the underuse of older actors on television, writing: 'Isn't it criminal to ignore stars like Spike Milligan, Patty Coombs, Eric Sykes, Benny Hill and Joan Sanderson? These old favourites should be working until they drop.'[26]

Thankfully the world of sitcoms once again came calling and Pat returned to the area of television she had always been most comfortable in. Between 1990 and 1992 she would make nine guest appearances in Warren Mitchell's series *In Sickness and in Health*, playing the assertive Mrs Carey. The role provided her with some unique comic moments, and when Alf Garnett was jilted at the altar by his long-term girlfriend Mrs Hollingberry it was Pat, in the opinion of Garry Bushell, who stole the show with her line: 'He told me 'e was well 'ung. It 'ung like an acorn between two crab apples.'[27] Writer Paul Mayhew-Archer worked with Pat on an episode of *An Actor's Life for Me* and would recall: 'Pat was lovely and I spent a lot of time gazing at her thinking, "Gosh. I'm working with Pat Coombs. She's a comedy legend." Of course what I should have been doing was asking her about all the things she'd been in and trying to get some stories out of her. But I didn't. She was a very funny lady, brilliant at playing people who are permanently perplexed.'[28] Further guest appearances followed with roles in *Roy's Raiders* and *Boon*.

According to journalist Hilary Kingsley, Pat's guest appearance in an episode of *Birds of a Feather* gave her 'the best, if the crudest line of her long career, lamenting the walk-out of Dorien's latest toy-boy-to-be: "Cor, I'd have strumped that Wayne till me dentures rattled!"'[29] It also gave Pat the opportunity to work alongside three of television's most popular actresses: Pauline Quirke, Linda Robson and Lesley Joseph. Pat considered Linda in particular to be 'a rare delight', and she would go on to work with Lesley in three series of *Queen of Romance* on radio.[30]

Birds of a Feather writer Gary Lawson would remember meeting Pat over the course of four or five days and recalled her as 'such great fun... one of the funniest people to have in the room and also a bit of a hero – her and Peggy Mount'. He revealed that she was given the part 'because she was almost playing against type... and that would be so unexpected'. Her infamous line also stuck in his head and he would remember her as 'one of those great comedy actors who underpinned whatever she did'.[31]

*

The 1990s were another decade of immense change for Pat, and as she approached her seventieth birthday inevitably she suffered the loss of many friends and colleagues. Funerals and memorial services became more and more frequent, although after getting 'hopelessly lost on the South Circular' in 1993 she wrote to her niece, Penny Hey: 'I hereby promise that I will never, <u>ever</u> attend a funeral again – 'cept my own!!'[32]

Pat resolutely continued working. *Noel's House Party*, in which she played the bizarre, organ-playing Prudence (Prue) Prendergast, was seen as giving her career a 'definite boost, and the chance for a new, younger audience to enjoy her talents'.[33] With regular features such as 'The Gunge Tank', 'Grab a Grand', 'Wait Till I Get You Home' and the popular character of Mr Blobby, the programme was a fixture for many families in the 1990s. Many celebrities were famously caught out by Noel Edmonds' 'Gotcha Oscar' including Barbara Windsor, Lionel Blair, Carol Vorderman and even Status Quo, and the series achieved viewing figures of up to 15 million.

One of the victims of 'The Gunge Tank' was actor Graham Cole (famous for his long-running role as PC Tony Stamp in *The Bill*) who became friends with Pat in later years, as did his daughter, Laura:

Laura became pen pals with Pat when she was eight years old until Pat became ill. She was such a beautiful lady and Laura became very emotional as she spoke about Pat's replies to her... one very special friend.[34]

Pat's role in *Noel's House Party* was limited and by no means artistically challenging, but she took to the role of Crinkley Bottom's finest needlewoman with great enthusiasm and even made public appearances as Prudence Prendergast dressed in a 'spectacular knitwear collection created for her by young designers, from a crazy cauliflower hat to a fluorescent harlequin dress'.[35] Pat's appearances in the series also allowed the next generation to see her live performances, as her great-niece Georgia Ross would remember:

Some of my fondest memories from childhood were going to watch auntie Pat recording TV and radio programmes, particularly *Noel's House Party* where we got to meet Mr Blobby.[36]

Having bemoaned the small screen in recent years, saying, 'Television is not the fun it was. These days it's all run by accountants and people who don't know,' Pat was delighted when *Celebrity Squares* returned in 1993 and she was able to appear on screen again with her dear chum, Bob Monkhouse. Despite her decades of performing, she remained as nervous as ever about working without a script: 'I remember when my agent rang me, originally I was full of fear and trembling because I always hated appearing as myself in the old days.'[37]

As Pat's television appearances began to noticeably slow down from the mid 1990s she nevertheless remained busy in other areas of the profession. Radio continued to bring some of her best work and – as ever – allowed her to take on a broader range of character roles. She played Daisy in a 1993 BBC adaptation of John le Carré's novel *A Perfect Spy* (the all-star cast including James Fox, James Grout, Brenda Bruce and Harriet Walter), drawing praise from the producer John Fawcett Wilson who was a 'great fan' of her work; and later in the decade she featured in *Babblewick Hall*, a Radio 4 sitcom, the cast of which also included Elizabeth Spriggs and Maggie McCarthy.[38] In 1996 she worked alongside Roy Hudd and Andrew Sachs in four episodes of *Educated Evans* (she was later cast to appear with Hudd and June Whitfield in their hit series, *Like They've Never Been Gone*), and thankfully continued to remain in demand for voice-over work into her seventies.

9
Battling on

'Be tolerant to all those little bent old ladies'

A WELCOME RETURN TO TELEVISION work came when Pat appeared in the first episode of the 1996 series *Valentine*, playing an old lady who refused to leave her home which is due to be demolished because her dog is buried in the back garden. Funded by Tom McCabe, the son of a bookie (at a cost of £250,000), Pat was persuaded to take a 50% pay cut in her own £3,000 appearance fee to help McCabe 'realise' his television dream.

The appearance should have marked a return to the small screen for Pat and propelled her career along for another decade. Although very much a veteran performer by the mid 1990s, there seemed to reason to think at the time that Pat, like her old friend Irene Handl, could not have continued working into her eighties. Alas her life and career were hampered by a sudden, sharp decline in health which would overshadow her remaining years.

By far the most dominating aspect of Pat's life from the mid 1990s until her death was her battle with the brittle bone disease osteoporosis. Prior to this Pat had enjoyed relatively good health. She had inherited a heart condition, a Coombs family trait, but this had been successfully controlled for years with medication; and she often suffered from chesty coughs (linked by her own admission to her lifelong heavy smoking habit) and a bad back, but generally speaking her physical well-being had rarely caused her any serious problems.

Although she had previously made her diagnosis of osteoporosis public knowledge, it was not until December 1997 that the true horror of her struggle with the disease was dramatically revealed in *The Sun* newspaper in an article written by her old friend, journalist Garry Bushell (whose television programme she had appeared in the previous year). Photographed in bed, wearing a nightdress and propped up by pillows, although she beamed for the camera Pat looked extremely thin and frail as she held a plate of prawns and chocolate biscuits, her 'favourite treat', brought to her by Bushell. She would later admit to me: 'Most of what he writes is absolutely true, tho' I wasn't born in Beckenham and as yet don't have blanket baths!!!'[1]

The article revealed that after filming a series of *Noel's House Party*, rather than attending the after-show party, she asked her driver to take her to casualty because of the intense pain she was suffering in her back following a chest infection. Admitting to six weeks of pain, Pat underwent X-rays which confirmed she was suffering from brittle bone disease. Having assumed she may have developed cancer, Pat was initially relieved at her diagnosis although in retrospect said she was wrong to have taken comfort in the news.

Pat would later disclose that the disease probably started in her forties saying, 'I once cracked my ribs just by moving an inch closer to Peggy Mount on a sofa... if I had a chest infection and a cough, I'd always be putting my back out. I also lost every tooth in my head before I was 30. They just crumbled away.'[2] The condition had never featured in Pat's family, although she did admit she was a prime candidate for the disease, having always been tall and thin, a heavy smoker and 'not one for exercise'.

Around the time of Pat's diagnosis it was thought that one in three women and one in twelve men over the age of fifty was affected by osteoporosis. Directly linked to genetics, a lack of oestrogen and heavy drinking and smoking, the disease can affect the whole skeleton, often leading to fractures to bones especially in the spine, hips and ribs.

Despite years of back problems, which involved regularly seeing a doctor, physiotherapists and osteopaths, Pat's illness remained undiagnosed until it was 'fairly well-developed' (even though she had undergone an X-ray after breaking her wrist during her time working on *EastEnders*). The condition primarily affected her spine, often in 'bouts' of about six weeks, and she would reveal: 'It starts slowly but I know that within a week I will be in terrible pain.' Some medication, including co-codamol, did bring Pat a degree of relief from the illness, but she also conceded that 'on some days I'm still no good for nothing'. Physiotherapy had no impact on her plight and she would reveal that at times her pain was so intense it made her scream.

Everyday tasks became increasingly fraught and she regretfully admitted: 'Little things do become a worry, especially when you're on your own. You'll be frightened to get in the bath in case you can't get out, or to empty the cat's litter tray. Even filling a kettle can make you nervous.'[3]

As a result of her illness Pat lost inches in height (she later stated a 'couple' of inches but in truth it was much more). Added to this was a dramatic weight loss. The combination of both factors left Pat looking frail and immensely aged. Although never a vain lady she became highly aware of the change in her appearance, on which she was the first to comment. Since Pat was 'of a generation who had their hair "set" weekly', visits to her flat by her long-term hairdresser remained a key feature and at least allowed her to look and feel better even during the periods in her final years when she was bedridden.[4]

From 1996 Pat was actively involved with the National Osteoporosis Society and as a result was happy to meet Camilla Parker Bowles (now Her Royal Highness the Duchess of Cornwall) whose mother, Rosalind Shand, had died from osteoporosis in 1994. Despite often receiving negative publicity in the press at this time, Camilla attended many events to support the society including helping to launch their 'Ten Famous Faces' £2.5 million fundraising appeal in January 1996. The *Daily Mail* featured an article reporting the event entitled 'Camilla Comes Out' showing Mrs Parker Bowles with a host of well-known faces including Maggie Philbin, the actress Moira Shearer, and Claire Rayner. Pat duly preserved the article for her niece Penny, writing at the top: 'Don't throw away! But don't we look awful?! I look like I've stepped out of my grave…!!!' and 'P.S. Camilla "Thing" was so nice!!'[5] Pat was indeed impressed with Mrs Parker Bowles and even mentioned the future Duchess of Cornwall in her letters to me.

Having spent so many hours helping others via her association with the Samaritans, Pat now found it helpful to talk to others about her condition. Ever humble, she was 'flattered' when the National Osteoporosis Society asked her to become a patron of the society; and during the final years of her life she did what she could to help their cause, including being present at fundraising events and helping to raise £100,000 in their 1998 Christmas Day appeal. Over twenty years later, Helen Kingman, an executive director of the society, would write: 'Pat Coombs was very supportive of the charity and I remember her with great fondness.'[6]

Her positivity remained outstanding and she rarely complained about her predicament, even at the times she was bedridden. 'Sometimes,' she once admitted, 'I put on a brave face to the outside world and moan only to the cats. But then I see something like a documentary on Great Ormond Street and I think, "Why am I even moaning when there's a little thing of two or three who's not even going to live?"' Having been forced to slow down considerably as a result of osteoporosis, Pat became more aware of her frailty and the disease she now had to live with, saying, 'To those who don't have it, all I can say is: Be tolerant of all those little bent old ladies.'[7]

Much of 1997 saw Pat largely bedridden or reliant on a wheelchair, yet she refused to give in. Despite her condition she still managed to make some public appearances at this time including being a guest at the unveiling of a Comic Heritage Plaque for Dick Emery. Seated in a wheelchair, she was photographed with Sir John Mills, Sir Norman Wisdom, Sir Harry

Secombe, Phil Collins, June Whitfield, Liz Fraser and Clive Dunn.

Throughout that year, however, her condition continued to give serious cause for concern, and she admitted that 'sense of humour or not it's become a 24 hour menace'.[8] She would report sadly, 'Day to day activities are becoming increasingly difficult – piles of unanswered mail for starters,' and she became ever more reliant on family members and friends, especially her nieces and Anne Harvey, to assist her on a daily basis.[9]

10

To Denville

'Totally unique'

IN JULY 1998 PAT WAS DELIGHTED to be well enough to return
to work in the BBC Radio 4 series, *Like They've Never Been
Gone*. Starring June Whitfield and Roy Hudd as Sheila Parr and
Tommy Franklin, a singing duo who had won the Eurovision
Song Contest in 1962 and were now attempting a comeback,
the series was written by Mike Coleman and first aired in
August 1998. Cast as Hetty, the couple's overworked domestic
help, Pat went on to appear in a further three series in 1999,
2001 and 2002. She received glowing reviews for her latest role
with *The Stage* writing, 'The couple were hilariously outshone
by their lackey, Hetty, who cruised the Internet as the self-
designated Cyber Vixen from Hell. Pat Coombs played hot
totty Hetty as if on speed – or in search of a spin-off series of
her own.'[1]

More than two decades after the series was first broadcast, Mike Coleman would recall his memories of Pat:

Warm, hilarious, genuine... these are the words that come to mind when I remember Pat.

I worked with her as the writer for four series of Radio 4's *Like They've Never Been Gone*. It was a sitcom about a veteran singing couple from the 1960s, whose one hit won the Eurovision Song Contest and whose career then bombed ... only to revive 40 years later for a TV advert.

Roy Hudd and June Whitfield, both also missed, played the couple and Pat was their not-so-loyal housekeeper; she was supposed to be a supporting character at first but it was clear after listening to the pilot that she had the rare talent of stealing many of the scenes she appeared in!

The first series was recorded without an audience – one reason being that Pat's osteoporosis meant she had to sit to deliver her lines. But it soon became apparent that this was no problem for Pat – she was as effective perched on a stool, grumbling and muttering ad-libs, as she would have been striding across the stage reading a script! So, after the first series was over, subsequent recordings were performed in front of a live audience.

Until Pat's funeral, I didn't realise that, as well as her acting career and her work for the National Osteoporosis Society, she also had a rare empathy with young people and willingly gave her time to listen to them and offer advice.

For a short time before Pat died, one of these young people was my daughter, Anna, who always insisted on coming along with me to recordings and also often with me to Denville Hall, the care home for retired theatricals where Pat lived and eventually died. (Other residents included Maurice Denham and Peggy Mount at that time – it could have been the base for a sitcom in itself!)

It was a sad shock for both Anna and me when, very shortly after what we realised would be the final recording of *Like They've Never Been Gone*, Pat sadly died of emphysema. When we recovered from the shock, the cast, myself and the producer Steve Doherty did briefly discuss recasting Pat or replacing the character completely –

but none of us really had our hearts in it and so that was the end of the series.[2]

Steve Doherty worked on all four series of *Like They've Never Been Gone*. Having grown up in an era when Pat was a constant fixture in the world of entertainment he regarded her as 'acting royalty' and a 'hoot'. Remembering her with affection as a 'lovely, lovely lady who could get a laugh out of almost anything', Steve was amazed at Pat's professionalism and comic timing and would recall that she was recommended for the role by her old friend and colleague, June Whitfield.[3]

In September 1998 Pat sent me one of her new publicity photographs from the series in which she was seen seated between June and Roy, wearing a dusky pink jumpsuit (an old favourite she had owned for more than a decade). 'I don't look as skinny as I feared!' she would write, 'but I am! And doctors are worried about my ongoing weight loss – 'specially as my appetite has improved. Never mind – I was able to do the series and must say the BBC were really kind and supplied transport and care on a daily basis… and I was spoilt rotten from every direction.'[4] In retrospect Pam Valentine admitted that it was probably the kindness and generosity of Roy Hudd that resulted in Pat's chauffeur-driven car to and from Broadcasting House, although this was never confirmed.

The year, by Pat's own admission, saw a general improvement in her 'day-to-day mobility' but she was disappointed when a specialist's report used the words 'degenerative' and 'more fragility of the hips'.[5] She revealed, 'I still have my weekly baths with the kind nurse (we're really pals now and I know her and her husband etc!) but not the dreaded BLANKET! 'Tis still sort of <u>in</u> the bath perched on a seat!'[6]

By December she was 'mobile-ish and coping fairly' well despite the death of 'beloved puss Rudy' who went to 'feline Heaven' in October of 1998 ('but 17 was pretty good eh?').[7]

In addition to *Like They've Never Been Gone*, Pat continued to do other work on radio, including joining Roy Hudd for a twelve-minute schools radio story in February 1999. She remained grateful for the opportunity and regarded such projects as a 'lot of fun and so good to get out and actually work within the hallowed halls of Broadcasting House'.[8] The second series of *Like They've Never Been Gone* was recorded in front of a live studio audience across six separate nights in May 1999. The thought of an audience pleased Pat, although she confessed: 'I dread the remarks when they see me. I'm so thin it's not true! And o' course my movement(s) will be slow! But I know any remarks will be out of kindness and concern... it's just that I'd give anything to replace some of the weight I've lost.'[9] Thankfully Pat had nothing to fear and just weeks later would write: 'Our first two recordings have gone really well... very friendly audience(s) and some cheering comments afterwards.'[10]

A recording on 26th May allowed me to meet Pat for the first time on one of my return visits to England from Australia. Accompanied by my godmother, Pauline Shields, I was in the audience for the show and later met Pat in the bar at Broadcasting House for a drink and chat. I was amazed by her extra long ('More' menthol) cigarettes, the way she slipped in and out of 'funny' voices and how effortlessly she conversed. During the course of our get-together a young boy, of approximately ten years of age, was dispatched by his father to get Pat's autograph. Not batting an eyelid she graciously signed the autograph book without putting her cigarette down; and we both giggled when the boy looked at me curiously, clearly wondering whether he should ask for my signature too.

I took Pat a present of a koala paperweight (later used, appropriately enough, to hold down her fan mail and named by Pat as 'Kenny') and a bottle of white wine. I received a letter (written at 6am the following morning) thanking me for my 'presence and wonderful present... I cannot thank you enough' and saying it "'twas nice to meet "Aunty" Pauline'.[11] The meeting cemented our friendship which continued until Pat's death.

Buoyed by new work projects, Pat tried her best to carry on. In June 1999 she attended a showbiz 'do' at the Hilton Hotel with Peggy Mount, given as a tribute to Ernie Wise. Pat would later write that they were among a 'sea of famous and familiar faces... so you can imagine all the gossip and "get togethering" we enjoyed'.[12] Further good news came regarding her health around the same time and she wrote, 'One bit of brighter news for me and this rotten bone disease... had another scan at the orthopaedic hospital last week and they told me the situation was 7% better than my last scan (Nov. '98)... brilliant eh?'[13]

As her health improved Pat began to make regular visits to Denville Hall, the actors' retirement home in Northwood, Middlesex. The main attraction there was her old friend and colleague Peggy Mount. Having first met during the filming of *Lollipop Loves Mr Mole* the two actresses subsequently became close friends during their times together on the set of *You're Only Young Twice*. It was very much a case of 'opposites attract', with Peggy being as 'difficult' as Pat was easy-going. The expression 'love-hate' is how June Whitfield summed up the relationship between the pair; and it was clear from Pat's letters that Peggy was often irascible, especially as her health and independence declined, and that Pat would regularly have to 'turn the other cheek' during Peggy's frequent outbursts.

Despite certain health issues in later years (including two hip replacements and having a pacemaker fitted) Peggy Mount had continued to work on prodigiously on stage throughout the 1980s and made occasional television appearances until as late as 1994. In the 1990s she was still appearing in annual pantomime performances, and in 1996 (the year she was awarded a long-overdue OBE) she received acclaim for her touching performance in Chekhov's *Uncle Vanya*, directed by Bill Bryden and co-starring Sir Derek Jacobi and Frances Barber. It was well known within the business that Peggy had struggled with poor vision for many years, the result of detached retinas. Gradually as she became older the issue grew worse. During her 1996 *Desert Island Discs* interview the indomitable star would admit to the problem but emphasised, 'I can see on the stage – as long as I know where everything is I'm perfectly all right.' She also conceded that friends and colleagues were very 'helpful' and that her lines were now learned with the assistance of a cassette tape player: 'A very dear friend puts it all on tape.' After a lifetime of reading lines on a page, Peggy found it difficult to adjust to this enforced way of learning, admitting that it was 'much easier to read the lines'. Having struggled through her performances in *Uncle Vanya* she went on to perform in one more pantomime production in the winter of 1996-97 before finally realising she could no longer carry on acting. By the beginning of 1997 she had lost most of her remaining sight, later saying, 'The audience had no idea. But… I lost my nerve… my greatest regret. It was always my wish to die working.'[14]

Going blind – and at the end of her life she was indeed registered as blind – was perhaps the most catastrophic event of Peggy's life and career. In some ways, the physical disability mellowed the often fearsome old lady, although others would argue that it made her famously short temper even shorter. Despite her affliction Peggy felt there was no reason why she shouldn't attend events, and her friend Ian Talbot remembers: 'She would always come to press nights – even when her sight was failing she would still turn up and she would give me a critique of what she thought of it. She was always absolutely charming with the public and I think when she lost her sight and people came up to her and still remembered her it really thrilled her.'[15] Actor Mark Curry (who was friends with Peggy during the last decade of her life) on the other hand felt that Peggy's loss of sight led to her feeling 'insecure' especially 'when meeting new people such as fans'.[16]

Before her hip operations (and prior to Pat's own decline in health) Peggy was often seen out and about with Pat at celebrity events, and actor Jeffrey Holland would remember Peggy – and her poor eyesight: 'We met at her various charity bashes with Patty Coombs… I'd go up to her and say, "Hello Peggy, how are you?" and she would say, "Who's that?" because of course she couldn't see… I'd say, "It's Jeffrey Holland," and she'd say, "Oh, hello darling!"'[17] Gillian Bryant, a stalwart supporter of the theatre and a fan of both Pat and Peggy's work, would also remember the pair together: 'I loved Pat and met her many times in later years – her wheelchair was pushed by Peggy. She had a saying about laughter being the best tonic.'[18]

With an almost total loss of vision, Peggy decided to sell her one-bedroom London flat and move to Denville Hall for full-time residential care. The privacy and safety of the home appealed to Peggy, as her long-time friend and frequent co-star, actress Eira Griffiths-Darton, explained: 'She was desperately aware of her vulnerability in that it was something she couldn't change – she knew there was a deterioration... it was a vulnerability that she couldn't tackle, she couldn't command, she couldn't boom out any more... Denville was a kind of cloak.'[19]

Peggy became one of Denville Hall's most memorable characters. During her early visits to the Hall, Pat had met actress Elspeth March on several occasions. The first wife of actor Stewart Granger (from 1938 until their divorce a decade later), March was a large lady and a large personality – a grande dame of British theatre whose distinguished circle of friends had included Laurence Olivier and Vivien Leigh. In Pat's words, Elspeth was very much 'the queen' at Denville Hall until her death in April 1999 at the age of eighty-eight. It was with some amusement that after March's death Pat would also say, 'Now we think Peg M. is stepping into *that* vacancy.'[20]

For her seventy-third birthday in August 1999 Pat received over seventy cards, letters and messages. Although she struggled to keep up with correspondence, she did her best and thanked me for a copy of the photograph we had had taken together: 'Lovely of you... but will ignore your skinny ole partner,' she would jokingly write shortly afterwards. At the same time Pat disclosed that Peggy Mount had been 'whipped into hospital' after suffering a stroke: 'We think and hope that it was a minor affair but, of all things, her speech has been badly affected... plus trouble with her right hand and other nasties like trouble swallowing.'[21] Peggy, famed for her deep bellowing voice, did return to Denville Hall and with daily speech therapy made significant improvements, although this would be the first in a series of slight strokes that would gradually weaken the spirited star.

Pat meanwhile continued to visit Denville Hall regularly; enjoying the entertainment provided there, including almost an hour of old music hall songs by 'dear Roy Hudd' shortly before he joined Pat again for a further series of *Like They've Never Been Gone*. Pat had admitted in the late summer of 1999 that 'God willing' she hoped to end her days at Denville Hall, 'as, when and IF the time comes'. Already in residence at the time were a host of well-known names from the acting profession including Maurice Denham, Doris Hare, Anthony Steel and Rose Hill.

Happily, Pat's health remained fairly stable at this time and she would comment, 'I'm O.K. – still slow-moving! And a silly coff! And still smoking!!!'[22]

On Sunday 24th October 1999 Pat returned to the stage for *An Audience with Peggy Mount and Pat Coombs*, hosted by actress Jean Fergusson at the Watermill Theatre, Bagnor, in aid of the National Animal Welfare Trust. In light of Peggy's recent stroke, Pat took to the stage alone, a prospect she found 'scary'. She would later write:

Can you imagine my nerves last Sunday?! Peg came, but for obvious reasons just couldn't take part (she sat in the front row) and thanks to a lovely, warm audience, and the friendliness and expertise of Jean Fergusson, I think all went well!! We chatted – unbelievably – for an hour and a half and were treated to a smashing hour of drinks, etc, before making for home.[23]

Peggy Mount's health temporarily did improve somewhat and in December 1999 Pat wrote, 'She's making a really good recovery and the voice is almost as normal <u>AND LOUDER</u>!'[24] Pat continued to visit as often as possible and was always made to feel welcome by staff and residents and their visitors alike.

Shortly after celebrating Christmas 1999 with her sister Pam and her family, Pat was the victim of a cruel robbery at her home. She would describe the incident in full:

> I was back here at home and robbed of my purse/wallet – by a BOGUS nurse-cum-carer, who was supposedly visiting a sick neighbour upstairs. <u>I</u> invited her in to make kind enquiries… she begged for a glass of water and in the short space of time it took to fetch it – the purse was gone! Isn't it evil? Luckily, not too much cash (£15+) but credit cards etc!!! I called the police because we remembered poor Muriel (upstairs) being similarly robbed several weeks ago – they won't catch the lady of course! But we've tried![25]

The first day of the new millennium was celebrated at Denville Hall, with Pat having stayed overnight in a private room to see in the new year with Peggy Mount. She had also penned one of her justly famous poems (see Appendix) to be included in a 'local archive thing'. Shortly afterwards she would spend eight hours in the local hospital with breathing difficulties. Having been given four oxygen treatments and antibiotics, she was later in hospital for further tests before admitting, 'They diagnosed asthma (never in my life before – smoker or no!) and pulmonary something or other!'[26] Regular chest infections, not helped by her heavy smoking, became part of Pat's everyday life in her later years. In 1997, when she first wrote to me, she was recovering from a 'particularly dreary attack of bronchitis' and she had almost grown to accept that such hindrances were the penalty for her ongoing addiction to nicotine.[27]

Despite her 'woes' Pat was delighted to be able to attend a voice-over session at the start of the new year for a cartoon series titled *Treasure*, working alongside Liz Smith; and was able to give regular gossipy updates on the residents of Denville Hall, including the plight of Althea Parker, the widow of Arnold Ridley (best known as Private Godfrey in the sitcom *Dad's Army*) who, as Pat wrote, 'developed Alzheimer's, out of the blue, a week or two back… doesn't know who or where she is and looks very poorly'.[28]

Visits to Denville Hall became more and more frequent and Pat decided to spend ten days there ('then they can spoil me rotten') to decide whether or not she would indeed like to move into the residential home. She admitted:

> I guess the time is coming, Andrew, when I make plans to move in permanently – while I still have the 'get up and go' to do it and while I can still enjoy the prospect. The family have been wonderful – but they have their own problems and life to cope with – without ME being an added burden! My saddest worry will be Nola-puss, but already several willing 'takers' – but it will break my heart I know.[29]

Her frequent trips to the retirement home also meant Pat was able to give regular updates on the health – and temperament – of Peggy Mount. A summary can be found below:

> Peg is recovering well… but her intolerant attitude towards some of the inmates is SO unkind and doing her no good at all… typical Peg, and has been ever since I knew her… silly, 'cos we all feel she is walking into another stroke. (7th December 1999)

> Am doing the usual daily activities… local shops – Denville in the evening – tho' thanks to Peg's intolerance (and alas, jealousy) the last two visits have been tricky… she stomped angrily out of the bar on

Monday saying (in THAT voice) 'I'm sick of seeing the back of you!!' just because I listen and chat to the others. It's norty isn't it?! And last night I never saw her at all ... everyone says 'O! Forget it and let her get on with it' but not so easy, is it? It'll blow over, I'm sure – but when <u>she's</u> ready!!! (5th April 2000)

Peg M. well back to her normal intolerant self. (19th June 2000)

Peg is recovered from her fall – but sort of frightened to move about without help (always to hand!). (16th August 2000)

She did recover very quickly [following a fall] and nothing was broken – but I think she lost confidence and was a bit afraid to walk without help... but she's fine once more and her usual, slightly difficult, self! (3rd September 2000)

Pat remained one of the country's most high-profile sufferers from osteoporosis and continued to raise awareness of the disease with regular interviews. Years earlier, her near contemporary in age, actress Beryl Reid, had also been diagnosed with the disease but her battle had been a very different one. After an enviable career on radio, stage, film and television, the BAFTA-winning actress was awarded an OBE in 1986, but by the time she reached her seventies was in near-constant pain from brittle bone disease, gradually becoming more and more bedridden at her unique home, Honeypot Cottage on the banks of the Thames in Berkshire. Two knee replacements towards the end of her life did little to help the once bubbly star, and her main relief from the crippling symptoms came via self-medicated brandy.

Despite her pain, Pat used her affliction to help others. It was somewhat typical of her generous nature that she was able to share her personal battle for a greater good. In June 2000 she discussed with Joanna Smyth her fight with brittle bones and the impact it had on her everyday life. She admitted her 'lovely nurse and wonderful cleaning lady' were a brilliant help – as too were her close relatives. Discussing the cause of the disease she would concede, 'I'm naughty because I still smoke, which is probably one of the reasons I got osteoporosis in the first place. Prevention is always better than cure, so smokers should stop if they can.'[30] She felt annoyed at her 'asthma' diagnosis and felt sure that it was a 'one-off episode', optimistically hoping that following a further visit to the asthma clinic in March 2000 her file would be closed. Despite her words of warning to others regarding the dangers of nicotine, ultimately Pat remained defiant and never gave up smoking.

By this stage Pat's health, thanks to painkillers and hormone replacement patches, was better than it had been for some time. Once again she was able to walk short distances, unaided, but admitted she struggled to stand for long periods. She had been unable to use a bus or the Tube for more than three years, but in the summer of 2000 was delighted to be able to drive once again and revelled in a return to a small degree of independence.[31] However, another emergency trip to hospital came in May of 2000, prompting a life-changing decision:

> … had a second health set-back with the scary breathing problem – and they kept me in the local hospital for 48 hours. So! To give us all peace of mind I am moving (full-time) to the actors' home in nearby Northwood – moving date July 1st but could be earlier if things move more quickly. Am <u>NOT</u> selling-up for several months, so in a sense will have <u>2</u> official addresses – and either or both will find me…! Will have a room number (and 'phone in room) and will keep you posted with numbers etc… I am truly looking forward to it all and it will be great to be with Peggy Mount and co. <u>No</u> restrictions as such and even SMOKING in designated areas… wot more could I want?! While I can still drive, will come and go to both 'homes'! and I know Puss-Nola will be cared for – so! They y'are!![32]

During the hot summer of 2000 Pat's letters revealed her anticipation regarding her impending move, which room she would be allocated and which items of her own furniture she would be able to take with her. Five days before moving into Denville Hall, Pat had been admitted to hospital again for five days 'with the asthma' but of her move said, 'I have NO regrets and am wonderfully well looked after in EVERY way and I can and do 'ave me white wine and me fag (so wot?!!)... and I am getting better-er!'[33]

After becoming a permanent resident at Denville Hall in the summer of 2000 she penned a poem commemorating her move to the actors' retirement home, a handwritten copy of which she sent to me:

'To Denville'

Denville 'All – up Norwood!
The place I wanted to be!
I'd passed the audition earlier
With a fag and a cuppa tea!

Now here I am all sorted
And settling in really well!
A lovely room with a magic bed (an 'adjustable', Andrew!)
And already stories to tell!

The smiling staff – my many pals –
Little bird in a cage 'n' all!
Then 'four paws Meg' the dog comes in
What's left? We can have a ball!

Just one little hiccup to worry –
My beloved 'Nola' the cat
But she's O.K. in a new home too
So that's the end of that!

Twice a day the bar's open
Twice a day we get drunk!
But no-one as yet has been banished
And no-one has done a bunk!

We laugh and enjoy the memories
Of wonderful times gone by
And tho' we fumble for names and stuff
We end the day with a sigh ...

Of relief and joy at where we are
And we know we are here to stay
The end of our time –
What more is there left to say?

I hope you all will tolerate
My funny ways and such!
I'll try to be a good girl
'Cos I love it all so much!

Bless you Denville – and thank you all for such a wondrous curtain
call!

Pat Coombs, Summer 2000

Despite her joy at moving to Denville Hall, many questioned
Pat's choice due to the presence of Peggy Mount. Obvious
parallels with their real-life relationship and the relationship
between their characters in *You're Only Young Twice* were
drawn, and some saw their friendship as life imitating art.
However, Pam Valentine rejects the notion that Pat was
browbeaten by Mount:

Patty was never bullied by Peggy Mount. Never. She would go along
with it so far, but she was her own person. She would laugh at some
of Peggy's outbursts and after she went into Denville she used to tell
me about some of the things Peggy would do – telling people to
'shuuut up' if they talked too much or purposely kicking someone's

> ball of wool as she walked across the room so it went to the far
> corner.
>   It was the right place for her to go, regardless of Peggy Mount.
> She could come and go, she could live her life.[34]

In the summer of 2000 Pat was interviewed for LAMDA's autumn newsletter concerning 'being a student 50 plus years ago – and the wondrous career I've had since', and thanked me for sending a batch of information regarding her numerous acting credits over the years ('I could not recall the many shows, series, etc, and there it all was!!').[35] Meanwhile she continued to delight in her work. Offers of voice-overs and television appearances were gladly accepted, including a chance to appear on Michael Barrymore's TV show, although health issues now made her particularly nervous about her abilities to perform and she would comment: 'I s'pose I sit on his sofa and answer questions... just wish I looked better for the studio audience (<u>SO</u> thin!) and only hope all goes well and that my new asthmatic breathing worry doesn't descend upon me.'[36] The episode in which Pat appeared also featured Darcey Bussell and the National Youth Ballet and was screened in December 2000. Radio commercials for London Buses allowed her another opportunity to do 'my usual off-cockney vocal thing' and brought 'some money in the bank';[37] and she was pleased to work with Martin Clunes, albeit briefly, in another commercial in which she said two words, 'Hello dear,' writing later: 'I gather money wise, it will make several quid eventually.'[38]

It became obvious through her letters that towards the end of her life Pat did have some concerns regarding her memory. When questioned about her appearance in the 1965 series *Barney is My Darling*, she would admit in May 2000, 'Still no recollection of the *Barney* sitcom – I tell you "Al… er… um… oh!… er CYBERS"?!! is en-route to add to my troubles! (several inmates @ D'ville suffer – 'tis SO sad, but I always feel it is worse for the looker-on…?)';[39] and four months later would further admit with candour: 'Honestly, my brain since coming here is ORFUL! Can't remember anything! And neither can any of us!! Ah well! One of the horrors of getting older!'[40]

Although there were never any real signs that Pat was suffering from anything other than slight general forgetfulness in her new environment, she became acutely aware of the horrors of dementia. Interestingly, at around the same time, Pat was encountered again by Chris Emmett who would recall her vagueness:

The final occasion when we met was at some function held at the Concert Artistes' Association in London's Bedford Street (also known as the Club for Acts & Actors). It wasn't a formal function, it was just a gathering of mutual chums to celebrate something. It could have been Sheila Steafel's 65th birthday or someone else's book publishing event (not Sheila's, that was years later after Pat died). Anyway, regardless of the actual event, I was wandering round, glass of wine in hand, chatting to various guests when I suddenly spotted Pat sitting alone at the side of the room. I quickly joined her and spent the next ten minutes or so happily chatting (having a catch-up) when there was a slight pause and Pat said through her usual beaming smile, 'I hope you don't mind me asking this but… who are you?'

I immediately laughed, thinking it was one of Pat's jokes, but then I realised by the almost pleading look in her eyes that she was serious. I was stunned and started to laugh it off, desperately wondering how I was going to handle this if true, when someone else grabbed me with one of those, 'Oh Chris, you must come and say hello to (whoever),' and I never got back to Pat. I caught a glimpse of her now and again still sitting alone but she'd gone by the time I was free again.

> So, once more, was Pat having a joke at my expense or was she
> really beginning to have memory problems? I only know that not too
> long afterwards I heard that she'd been admitted to the Denville Hall
> Nursing Home... [41]

Despite the indignities and trials of growing older, Pat remained extremely pleased with her new home and the comforts it offered. Having spent a lifetime being frugal and allowing herself no real luxuries she now found herself surrounded by more than she could ever have wished for. Just months after moving to Denville Hall she would write:

> We really are lucky – absolutely everything is laid on, including daily
> laundry, help with baths, bed making, room cleaning... even floral
> arrangements when we are lucky enough to receive them! What
> more could I want? Great meals (in your room if you want them) –
> attractive grounds – chairs outside and the bar, etc, etc... TV sets in
> every room and of course me and one or two others have got our
> 'magic beds' from home – 'craftmatic-adjustmatic' or whatever!
> Plenty of bathrooms, toilet and showers in some rooms (I have!)...
> a kitchen in 2 places for making yet more tea/coffee/Horlicks if you
> want it! I do!! I wake so early that I creep along the corridor @ 5am
> – sit in a little 'smoking area' outside kitchen and enjoy a crack o'
> dawn fag and cuppa and COFF!!! Ah! Happy days. Long may I feel
> the benefit and enjoy the company of some delightful old pals... [42]

Her daily routine involved rising early (4.30am was not uncommon) and enjoying a series of cups of tea. Her letters were often written at the 'crack o' dawn' and she admitted life at Denville was quite 'busy' and enjoyable. An endless array of activities, concerts and visitors kept Pat occupied while the protective nature of the staff allowed the famous occupants to be shielded from any unwelcome media attention. Pat clearly adored being a resident at the exclusive actors' retirement home. Her only bone of contention was with the former heart-throb film actor Anthony Steel.

Steel, six years Pat's senior, began his career following active service in World War II. Trained at Rank's 'Charm School', he appeared in a succession of films from the late 1940s and in 1952 had been voted Britain's fourth most popular actor. By the mid 1950s he was one of the Rank Organisation's highest-paid actors, and in 1956 he married the Swedish actress Anita Ekberg (they divorced in 1959). Despite much media attention at the time, Steel's career as a 'B' grade film star was relatively short-lived. Although he continued to act sporadically throughout his life (he made a final television appearance in *The Broker's Man* in 1998), a drink problem hampered his career and by the 1990s he was a virtually penniless recluse, living on a state pension and housing benefits.

According to actress Muriel Pavlow, Steel 'still maintained his charm… He always looked after the elderly ladies, making sure they had a chair to sit on, little things like that, which endeared him to them.'[43] His apparent charm was never evident to Pat, to whom, for some unknown reason, he took an instant dislike. Like Pat, Steel was a chain-smoker and it was inevitable that their paths should cross because there was only really one area of the nursing home where residents were permitted to smoke.

Pat admitted of her nemesis, 'HE TRULY HATES ME!!' Although she promised to divulge further details of his animosity in person ('tell you when next see you'), her letters still revealed some of his verbal abuse and she wrote, 'He told me I looked "like a 3rd rate brothel keeper" the other day.' Needless to say Pat was shocked by his remarks ('ME?! I ask you!!'),[44] later describing him as 'yukky' and questioning his dislike of her: 'Anti-me?? Why?!!'[45]

In his day Anthony Steel had been extremely handsome, with a head of thick wavy hair and perfect Hollywood smile. By the age of eighty his hair remained as fulsome as ever, albeit lily white, and he sported a matching beard. His once gleaming smile, however, had disappeared. By the 1980s a lifetime of chain-smoking and heavy drinking saw his teeth badly decayed. He had undergone extensive and expensive dental work in his mid sixties, but a decade later this had collapsed. Shortly after arriving at Denville he was fitted for a full set of dentures.[46] It was a constant source of amusement to Pat that the former heart-throb was now toothless, and she would happily say to friends, 'He's got no teeth!'

From her earliest days Pat herself had struggled with her own teeth and wore a full set of dentures for the majority of her adult life. She was therefore well placed to gently tease her fellow resident who, unlike Pat, was well known to be vain. Penny Hey, Pat's niece, would recall that despite her aunt's lifelong frugality she did spend large amounts of money on dentures, but never seemed to find any that she was particularly happy with; they were often uncomfortable, and – especially in her final years, as her weight decreased rapidly – would need regular adjustment. Pat's great nieces and nephews still remember her habit of 'spitting out' her dentures but managing, miraculously, to pull them back into her mouth using only her lips. It was the kind of act guaranteed to fascinate and amuse young children.[47]

By November 2000 Pat would write: 'The sad Mr Steel seems to be confined to his room and I can't help but feel relieved…

they don't tell us why, but we know he HATES the winter and we also know that he is suffering from cancer.'[48] It was with girlish delight that Pat informed Pam Valentine that Steel had been moved 'downstairs' at Denville Hall:

> She used to ring me a lot when she was in Denville and tell me all the goings-on and what was happening.
>
> Anthony Steel was there. He'd lost his teeth – and lost everything – and just hated Patty. He was vile to her. She told me a particular episode where he went into a bar where you could smoke and he called her dreadful things. I said, 'Patty, you can't let him get away with that. You've got to go and tell someone,' and she said, 'Nope! I'm not going to.' And I said, 'Why not?' and she said, 'Because they've moved him down to the ground floor and that means he's going to die!'[49]

Of course Pat was right. Anthony Steel died at Denville Hall, from lung cancer, on 21st March 2001 at the age of eighty. Pat was left alone in the smoking room – and peace reigned.

As well as making new friends at Denville Hall, Pat was delighted by visits from many long-standing friends and colleagues including Barry Burnett, Pam Valentine and Anne Wood who would remember Pat with affection: 'I loved her and thought she was the loveliest person. We stayed friends and she used to share stories about Peggy Mount. Even when she was getting so ill, she still had the twinkle in her eye.'[50] Steve Doherty and Mike Coleman, from *Like They've Never Been Gone*, also called on Pat and Steve would remember the sound of Peggy's booming voice, which he believes grew even louder when she became blind, and accidentally walking into Maurice Denham's room![51] Family members too were a constant delight to Pat, including her sister Pam, her nieces and their families; and she also urged me to visit, writing, 'PLEASE come and see us at Denville… visitors welcome at any time! Plus bar and good food! Metro tube-line from Baker Street… and I can pick you up. TA-RA TOY BOY! O! They will be jealous @ D'Ville!!' [52]

Actress Lisa Bowerman – who photographed a beaming Pat at Denville Hall not long before her death – was also a welcome visitor and remembers Pat well:

> She was really lovely, and a good laugh – she tried her best to keep her spirits up whenever she could, despite battling poor health latterly.
>
> We had some good chats about acting (she also taught I think) where we'd have a good moan about poor diction!! There's a little room at the end of a corridor at Denville (actually the one pictured in the colour ones), lovingly known as Pat's room, as that was where she'd inevitably be found having a quick smoke! [53]

A string of further bereavements had hit Pat during the 1990s, including the death of her former sister-in-law June in 1997, and many of her colleagues including Terry Scott, Marti Caine and Rod Hull; and inevitably friendships formed at Denville Hall were also severed by the passage of time. Although she only knew her fairly briefly, Pat was delighted to meet Denise ('Diz') Sinclair, who was a resident at the home from June 1999 until her death in September 2000. Diz had acted 'briefly in her youth' so it was via her daughter, actress Sue Sinclair and her work in theatre and television, that she was allowed to take up residence at Denville. During the course of her visits to see Peggy Mount, Pat and Diz had become firm friends and Pat felt the loss of one of her 'favourite people' intensely:

> Denise Sinclair was a lovely lady and would've been a very young 80 Xmas week. She and I were great pals – she had a wonderful (rude!) sense of humour and every evening we lingered in the smoking room (tho' she stopped years ago) with our pet drinks – me with white

wine and Denise with BISHOP'S FINGER (a lager!) and/or red wine and we struggled with the *Sun* crossword! She had a great family too – son, Adrian, and daughter Sue and grandchildren – Sue is in show biz and doing very well with commercials etc.

Almost a decade after she vowed never to attend another funeral, Pat admitted that she 'just couldn't face' Denise's funeral but was in attendance for the 'smashing send off' Denville Hall gave her afterwards.[54] In 2019 Sue Sinclair would recall her memories of Pat and the friendship she enjoyed with Sue and her mother:

My mother, Diz, went into Denville Hall in the late 90s. Peggy Mount was already an (unwilling) resident and Pat visited her regularly. We always looked forward to Pat's arrival – she was witty, amusing, lively and great fun to be with. It was striking that Pat's relationship with Peggy frequently mirrored the relationship their characters had in film and television. Peggy was strong and could be overbearing and Pat, more often submissive and acquiescent. In time Pat could no longer live independently despite the solid and loving help she had from her relatives so Pat moved into Denville Hall.

Pat, Peggy and my mother enjoyed one another's company hugely. The stories were legend, the laughs frequent and dirty. I remember them as the three naughty girls of the house and they were in fact told off for some misdemeanour toward another resident. We would serve and pay for their drinks in the bar before supper on the understanding they'd 'only had one' if they stumbled to their dinner table.

There are two (often repeated, I'm sure) theatre stories which Pat told. She worked with Charlie Drake who had an eye for the gorgeous blonde chorus girls. One day he asked a girl, 'What would you say to a little fuck?' to which the chorus girl replied, 'Hello little fuck;' and I clearly remember Pat lovingly recounting the tale of her and Peggy's stint with Rod Hull and Emu. Apparently cast notes were given by a naked Rod in his dressing room after the show. Pat told us with glee: 'Ooh, it was like a shrivelled walnut!'

> When my mother died and then Peggy died, we still visited Denville. Pat and another resident we had come to know were friends and we loved seeing them. It was sad when Pat died but we were honoured to be at her funeral. If I see her face in my mind, I think cheeky, mischievous and always making me smile. That would be her legacy. [55]

Ever cheerful, Pat continued to revel in visits from family members, including a 'new' great-nephew at the end of 2000, and from her cherished cat, Nola, who had settled into a new home but was brought to Denville to see her old mistress (and even got 'plonked on Peg's lap and she is NOT an animal person!'). Meanwhile new residents arrived at Denville Hall, including Linda Polan, Sheila Keith and Michael Deacon, described by Pat as 'all <u>very</u> THEATRE!!!' [56] Even at the end of her life and career it seemed that Pat was categorised as a certain 'class' of actor; and, despite being generally much-loved within the profession, not all were enamoured of her charms. Dame Patricia Routledge, best known as Hyacinth Bucket in television's *Keeping Up Appearances*, in Pat's opinion was one such example and she would write: 'I met her for the first time several years ago and couldn't believe her stand-offishness… tell you when I see you.' [57]

Pat was clearly aware of the unusual mix of residents, from all walks of the entertainment industry, and after a visit from her sister Pat would write, very tellingly, 'Pam is always slightly anti-showbiz folk… says they are insincere and over the top! Well – 'tis true of some of them but many, many more are a delight – think I.' [58] Regular 'open days' at Denville allowed Pat to meet many 'famous faces' including Richard Attenborough, who was Patron of the actors' home for many years before becoming a resident there with his wife, the actress Sheila Sim.[59] She also continued to accept occasional social invitations, and having attended June Whitfield's 75th birthday party (and the launch of her autobiography, *...And June Whitfield*) in November 2000, Pat was again reunited with her old friend for another series of *Like They've Never Been Gone*.

After an absence of some four years since her last acting role on television, Pat would travel to Birmingham to play Irene Morris, a lady seeking answers to her past, in the popular and long-running series, *Doctors*. The role had the added bonus of requiring no walking for Pat, since all her scenes were filmed in a hospital bed, and she would write later that her character 'died in bed'. It was slightly ironic, after a lifetime spent working in television comedy, that Pat ended her small-screen career in a dramatic production. It was perhaps a sign of changing times, since a number of veteran actresses known for comic roles were being allowed to broaden their horizons by appearing in more serious roles. Although purely speculative, it would have been interesting to see if Pat would have taken on further similar work, had she lived longer.

Undeniably Pat's range as an actress, by her own choice and lack of confidence, was never fully explored. Anne Wood would recall that Pat always shied away from playing 'straight' roles:

> She was always the one who used to hide her light really. I remember Tom Conti doing a one-hander play – it was about a man at the end of his life – they came up with one about a woman and they offered it to Pat but she wouldn't do it. It terrified her. She did not like theatre... She was shy but a very clever actress, really clever – she understood – but she never trusted her instinct and lacked that brash confidence.[60]

Writer Gary Lawson also admits, 'I would have liked to have seen her in straighter parts... because when you're that good, you're that good.'[61]

Despite her invitation for me to visit Denville to discuss the possibility of working together on 'the book that never was' (her autobiography), the last time I saw Pat Coombs was on 9th February 2001 following a recording *of Like They've Never Been Gone* at Broadcasting House in London. Our 'date' had been arranged via a series of telephone calls – one of which involved Pat using a telephone redial system and inadvertently speaking to my grandmother, Mary Ross, instead of me. Their conversation (initially quite confused!) became a source of much amusement for some time afterwards.

At the end of the recording Pat sat waiting for me on the stage, propped up by a large cushion, until the audience had departed. I was escorted to her by a member of staff. Now tiny, painfully thin and much frailer than she had been at the time of our first meeting, she nevertheless sparkled with life and wit. I was greeted with an affectionate kiss directly on the lips – no showbiz 'air kisses' for this lady, I remember thinking at the time. Walking slowly but unaided, her breathing difficulties all too apparent (and not helped by the fact she had forgotten her inhaler), Pat led me through a series of warren-like corridors in an attempt to find the green room. After opening a cupboard door we were 'rescued' by Roy Hudd and moved backstage for a buffet supper and champagne. Via Pat, I was introduced to the legendary June Whitfield (and her daughter, actress Suzy Aitchison) and had conversations with the delightful Roy Hudd and his charming wife, Debbie Flitcroft. Sitting throughout the occasion, Pat was full of chatter and clearly on a high following her live performance. She would later write that our second meeting was 'smashing' and went on to say, 'I for one would love it if you return to England.'[62]

During the autumn of 2001 Peggy Mount's health began its slow and final decline. It was around this time that actress Zulema Dene, who had worked with Peggy on television, would once again encounter her former colleague while visiting another friend at Denville Hall. She would remember, with sadness, this closing stage of Peggy's life:

> She was having lunch and was very depressed because she had lost her sight. I felt that Peggy who had lived for her work now felt there was nothing left for her. When I left Denville that day I felt immensely sad that this woman with such talent and drive was just waiting for death.[63]

By November the indomitable star was bedridden. On 3rd November she had her Last Will and Testament altered, appointing a new firm of solicitors to carry out her final wishes, but was too frail even to sign the new codicil (the changes were instead read to her and signed on Peggy's behalf). In her final days, suffering from bronchopneumonia and congestive cardiac failure, she slipped in and out of consciousness. Her devoted friend, Eira Griffiths-Darton, remained a constant support and rarely left Peggy's side.

Peggy Mount died peacefully in her sleep at Denville Hall during the early hours of 13th November 2001. She was eighty-six years old.

Pat and Peggy had been friends for thirty years. Having spent so much time together, especially in the last couple of years of Peggy's life, her death was a deep blow for Pat whose own health issues were now beginning to cause increasing concern.

The last communication I had with Pat was via an email sent from the office at Denville Hall in the early spring of 2002. I had sent my usual birthday card and letter, a further letter of condolence following the death of Peggy Mount in November and a card at Christmas time (2001), but tellingly had not heard back from my famous friend. Sensing that Pat was now very ill, and not wishing to trouble her via telephone, I contacted Denville Hall to enquire after her. I duly received a reply from the manager of the actors' retirement home thanking me on Pat's behalf for getting in touch. My email had been read to her and she sent the following, very typical, reply: 'Bless you for thinking about me. I haven't been too well recently but getting better-rer!!'

Sadly Pat's optimism only hid the seriousness of her condition. She had been aware for years that her battle with osteoporosis could lead to death but consistently tried 'not to think about getting worse'. Her sense of humour had sustained her through many difficult patches and she considered her own comedic personality 'an absolute boon' saying, 'I inherited mine from my mother and it does you through thick and thin.'[64] Although her mother's gift never left her, Pat was now gravely ill. Typically, she managed to keep the truth of her predicament from close relatives, including her niece Penny Hey who remembers her aunt telling her she was being treated for an 'infection' in her ulcerated foot. Making light of what must have been intense suffering, ever the actress, Pat continued to put on a show of stoicism until the very end of her life.

As 2002 progressed, amazingly offers of work continued to come in – and continued to be accepted. Throughout the interviews she gave discussing her battle with osteoporosis Pat maintained she had no intentions of ever retiring – and she never did. In February a fourth series of *Like They've Never Been Gone* was recorded at Broadcasting House, and Roy Hudd wrote at the time: 'The real star of the show is our house-keeper/minder-cum-hitwoman played by the one and only Pat Coombs. Patty hasn't been too well and out of the game for some time but now she's back with a vengeance and just as offbeat and brilliant as ever. June and I love working with this great gal.'[65]

Writer and broadcaster Matthew Sweet was in the audience for the recording of Pat's final series of *Like They've Never Been Gone*, by which time she was once again reliant upon a wheel-chair, and would later write about her performance, before, during and after the recording:

> She glides into the room like a Georgian State dancer. Between her long fingers smoulders one of those skinny cigarettes that used to be advertised on the back of *Woman and Home*. She is more of a surprise than Whitfield and Hudd. The London Academy of Music and Dramatic Art (where she was a contemporary of Diana Dors) has smoothed and deepened the Camberwell vowels of her child-hood to something more appropriately actorly. But as soon as she is called upon to deliver a line – particularly one containing the expression 'ooh-err' – the familiar transpontine rasp returns.

Although heavily medicated and tired, Pat 'beamed happily' and remained a consummate professional throughout the occasion. Despite age and illness she had lost none of her comic timing. Steve Doherty would remember that Pat would conserve her energy throughout the day to deliver sparkling performances and despite suffering from shortness of breath (made worse if she got a fit of the giggles) managed to 'deliver the goods' throughout each recording.[66] Matthew Sweet left the recording suitably impressed and considered Pat, Roy Hudd and June Whitfield to be 'masters at work'.[67] Pat's final work on radio would be broadcast posthumously in the summer of 2002.

It was around this time that television documentaries on 'legends' of British comedy began to become popular. Featuring interviews with family, friends and colleagues, a spate of such programmes (on popular figures such as Sid James, Kenneth Williams, Diana Dors and Les Dawson) began to appear, and quite rightly Pat was invited to be interviewed regarding her beloved friend Dick Emery for the *Heroes of Comedy* series for Channel 4. Immaculately made-up and sporting a fresh coiffure for the occasion, Pat wore a vibrant pink turtleneck sweater and glasses, to recall her frequent co-star with affection. Her voice was noticeably deeper and raspier than ever ('like the noise of somebody trying to sandpaper a housebrick' according to Matthew Sweet),[68] and her oversized dentures gleamed in the studio lights. The episode was screened for the first time in April 2002. It was Pat's last television appearance and fittingly the final words in the programme were left to her.

Gradually the indomitable actress became weaker and slightly more vague. She was warned by staff at Denville not to walk around barefoot and in her final months was invariably seen wearing white wraparound slippers to protect her feet. Eventually she was admitted to a local hospital. Whilst there she was dramatically told that she would need to undergo the amputation of a foot in order to save her life. Pat telephoned her niece Penny in a state of panic, insisting that she needed to leave the hospital immediately. Adamantly refusing surgery, she returned to Denville Hall, never to leave again. In the last couple of weeks of her life Pat 'took to her bed' and as a result was unable to smoke cigarettes for the first time in her adult life. Without the comfort of her beloved 'More menthols' and favourite 'tipple' her final days were distinctly uncharacteristic.

On the evening of 24th May Pat was visited by her devoted nieces, Penny and Sally, at Denville Hall. When the two sisters returned the following morning Pat was heavily medicated and more or less unconscious. On the afternoon of 25th May 2002, Pat Coombs died peacefully, 'from complications arising from emphysema', at the age of seventy-five.[69]

*

Pat's death was announced by the BBC who described her as 'one of Britain's great character actresses' and a 'stalwart of comedy'. Newspaper obituaries quickly hailed her as 'one of the unsung talents of comic acting', an actress who 'made the role of the stooge her own, specialising in the portrayal of the eternal downtrodden female',[70] a 'TV Comedy Legend'[71] and 'Comedy Queen'.[72]

Dame Barbara Windsor, Pat's co-star on several occasions, would say at the time, 'She was one of the most lovely people I knew and a complete joy to work with,'[73] and speaking about Pat's involvement with *EastEnders* would add: 'She was incredibly popular with all the cast. This is a great loss.'[74] Barry Burnett, still Pat's agent at the time of her death, said, 'She was a TV comedy pioneer. A queen of comic timing,' while Roy Hudd would describe her as 'a one-off'[75] and 'the female Tommy Cooper... a wonderful character actress... totally unique'.[76] Linda Edwards, director of the National Osteoporosis Society, would add: 'In spite of the terrible pain she endured with her osteoporosis, she was always making a joke to make me laugh when I visited her. She was determined to help others avoid the pain she'd endured and was thrilled when her Christmas appeal letter raised £100,000 for research, the best single appeal result we'd ever had.'[77] Anne Hardy, to whom Pat had been a long-standing friend, would say: 'She was a really good laugh and was a very kind person. She used to say she did not have a lot of glamour, but she could make them laugh.'[78] Almost twenty years after Pat's death her long-term pen pal and friend Pat Morris would write: 'I still miss Patti and those daft phone calls – and my overwhelming memory is of a charming and elegant lady who loved cats, with a terrific sense of humour and FUN.'[79] Chris Emmett, who regarded Pat as somewhat 'enigmatic', would later say: 'We shared the same sense of humour and she was great company. I adored the woman and I was lucky to have known her,'[80] while Steve Doherty would write: 'She loved making people laugh and people loved her for it. A performer proudly of "the old school", I have the fondest memories of our time working together in studio and gossiping together in the grounds of Denville Hall.'[81]

Pat's funeral took place at 11.45am on Friday 31st May at Breakspear Crematorium in Ruislip. The service was conducted by the Reverend David Dickinson who said that Pat had 'brought sunshine and laughter into our lives'.[82] More than one hundred mourners gathered to say goodbye including Tony Blackburn, Des Rayner, Lady Katie Boyle, Penny Morrell (wife of actor George Cole), and actress and Denville Hall patron Lalla Ward.

Irene Sutcliffe led the readings and said, 'Thank you for the laughs, Patty. I shall miss you.'[83] Uplifting songs including

'Bring Me Sunshine' and 'Somewhere Over the Rainbow' from *The Wizard of Oz* were played during the service as Reverend Dickinson remembered Pat with fondness saying: 'The smile on her face never changed. She was not the most outgoing of people. It would take her friends a week to persuade her to go to a party, and it took all night for them to persuade her to go home.'[84]

The poem *The Life That I Have* by Leo Marks, famously recited by Virginia McKenna in the 1958 film *Carve Her Name with Pride*, was a favourite of both Pat and her mother, and was read during the service.

> The life that I have
> Is all that I have
> And the life that I have
> Is yours.
>
> The love that I have
> Of the life that I have
> Is yours and yours and yours.
>
> A sleep I shall have
> A rest I shall have
> Yet death will be but a pause.
>
> For the peace of my years
> In the long green grass
> Will be yours and yours and yours.[85]

After a lifetime of being famously 'careful' with her money, Pat left a sizeable estate of £354,813 (net value £349,854). Her one-bedroom flat in Wendela Court, consisting of a fourteen-foot lounge/diner, similar sized master bedroom, kitchen and bathroom, had sold for £132,500 in March 2001, substantially topping up her savings.[86] In her will (dated 3rd March 1999) Pat left specific bequests of various items of jewellery (including her mother's wedding ring, a diamond solitaire and the green chrysoprase ring she was often photographed wearing), paintings, books (namely her grandfather's Charles Dickens collection), and cash sums to her nieces and godchildren. A sum of £5,000 was left to care for any feline companions she had left at the time of her death while Anne Harvey received £30,000, along with Pat's 'Adjustomatic orthopaedic bed and small oak bookcase'. Pat left a specific request that her executors purchase a wooden garden seat with inscribed brass plaque to be situated within the grounds of Wendela Court. A sum of £1,000 was left to the National Osteoporosis Society while the remainder of her estate was divided between her sister Pam and two of her nieces.

Almost twenty years have elapsed since the death of Pat Coombs. Since then many of her colleagues and contemporaries have also passed away and a new generation of actors and actresses has emerged. Yet despite the passage of time Pat Coombs does indeed, in the words of Roy Hudd, remain a 'one-off'. There has been no one to replace her – or even come close. Her looks, mannerisms, voice and talent were unique. Pat's place in British comedy history is secure. Those who knew her can surely imagine her reaction to remaining one of the best-loved character actresses of her generation: Pat would have giggled and slipped into one of her 'funny voices'… and said quite simply, 'ooh-err'.

Bestest love – write again soon – Patty X

Appendix
A selection of poems by Pat Coombs

'Miss Muffet'

North Country – Old Version

Young Muffet, wi'a bite o'lunch,
Some sandwiches of spam for brunch,
Sat ont' muck 'eap so it seems,
Weavin' luscious, rosy dreams!
Came t' spider fat and lazy –
Eee! 'er visions – they turned 'azy!
Wi' a yelp 'er crumbs she scattered –
Spider left – 'is dreams were shattered

Variable Welsh

Gwynneth – she was very sweet
Took some junket for to eat.
Poor girl didn't see the spider,
There'e was now – right beside 'er!
'Why 'allo! Miss Muffet' said 'e,
'Spare a little, please for me?'
'No!' cried Gwynneth, 'That I won't do!'
She was gone (*click fingers*) like that – Now look you!
(Hi-De-Hi 'Allo Campers!!)

Cockney – New Version!

Miss Muffet – on a *Tuffet*?! COR WOT A LARF!
She was sittin' pretty in 'er marble barf!
Sippin' champagne from a cut-glass bowl,
When a bloody great spider come up the 'ole!
Out shot the plug with an almighty slurp,
She stifled a yawn – and a big burp!
But she rang the Ole Bill in double quick time,
And that's the <u>True</u> tale of this old nursery rhyme!
Know wot I mean?!

Irish – New Version

Dis is an Irish story – told with joy,
Concernin' O'Muffet – a wee Irish boy!
He was sittin' pretty on his potty –
Eatin' taties – fried and hotty!
When dis froightful t'ing just happened by –
'Twasn't a spider and 'twasn't a fly,

Just a knobbly shillelagh, shiny and new –
And that's how the Irish got into a stew!

Scottish – New Version

On a broad, bright, moonlit night,
Miss Jean Brodie was rolling tight!
Singing and laughing and being that frisky,
She opened her umpteenth Scottish Malt Whisky!
But a spider who was passing by,
Fancied a wee drop – and why not? Och aye!
He leapt upon her, casting his spell –
And at last Miss Jean Brodie stumbled and fell!
It wasn't the shock of his lager and lime
'Twas just that Jean Brodie had discovered her prime!

For Fun! U.S. Of A.!

I'm a Yankee Doodle Dandy Spider –
From de Bronx… my name is Schneider!
I clocked dis Muffet on de Great White WHEY
Stuffin' herself with hamburgers – Oy VEY!
I fancied one myself – O.K.?
So right beside her I did lay!
She upped and left at one helluva pace!
And what was I left with?… EGG on my FACE!

Patty Coombs, 1985

Patty's Pome!

What does Xmas mean to <u>me</u>? Now that I'm well past 63?!
I don't no more 'ang my stocking up (I don't!!)
At the end of my comfy bed,
I don't no more leave a saucer and cup
For Santa to be watered and fed!
No! I sit alone with my memories of days so long gone by
Of carols, kids and church bells – and snow from out the sky…

So – what <u>do</u> I 'ave now I'm all alone –
Apart from my cats and my thoughts –
The odd mince-pie with custard,
And… a bag of Liquorice Allsorts!

They've always been my favourite (they 'ave!)
Next to Cadbury Fruit and Nut!
They've got a kind of flavour
You can tell with both eyes shut

Tho' my cats aren't very keen on them – <u>No-o</u>!!
(They sit and watch me chew)
They know that given long enough
I'll weaken!… Wouldn't you?

So out come my bits of turkey –
And bits of stuffing too!
They even like the bread sauce
And all the giblets… <u>Coo</u>! (Well, it rhymes!)

'Ere!! We used to live near Croydon – I'll bet you didn't know?
But Dad worked in the High Street; many moons ago!
And sister Pam went schooling in Coloma's hallowed halls
Tho' I went to school in Beckenham and it was all a load of
    B…s! (Well it was!!)

I say! We settled in West Wickham
Right next to Springpark Woods –
The Doodle-bugs kept falling there…
And we all wore pixie hoods!

O' memories of yesteryear
They keep comin' back…
My Dad he was in the Home Guard –
So 'e was all right, Jack!

Then – our Mum went and died at Xmas:
Her favourite time of year…
But I like to think she knew just that –
And I hope that she can hear…
What Xmas means to <u>me</u>?
I've got baubles – I've got the tree –
I've got memories – and I've got the key…
It means – God Bless the Familee – !!

Patty Coombs, December 1992

Patty's Pome!

Born and bred in London – Harrow was just a name –
I grew up in East Dulwich – which doesn't sound the same
And moving ever southwards, we eventually reached the coast
Till finally we Coombsies settled in a spot we loved the most

A little village called Lindfield – far away from the madding
    crowd
Peaceful, pretty and quiet – with an air wot made me proud!
And then, well into my forties, I travelled north of the Thames
To find myself on the edge of 'the Hill', one of England's gems.

So… for twenty-five years, me and pussies galore
Have lived happily together on the ground floor
Of a home and garden rich with blooms –
A suitable place for ole Patty Coombs

Then trouble reared its ugly head
And I found myself trapped – indoors in bed…
Crumbly bones had come my way –
And, with alarming speed, poor health held sway

But with friends and neighbours old and new
And – bless her – caring Doctor Sue,
I've kept my sanity all intact –
Enjoying the Orange Badge… and that's a fact!

With help at hand in every way,
I've lived to fight another day!

Under Stanmore's orthopaedic banner –
Periodic tests and the old bone scanner!

The C.A.B. with advice for all –
Bridget Johnson forever on call…
Kind nurse Jo and the weekly bath –
Always a smile and always a laugh…

I've many to thank for living in 'Arrer –
Including my postman, whose name is Fara ..!
ENUFF! ENUFF! You'll be bored to tears –
But thank you all for allaying my fears

HARROW BE THY NAME,
THY KINGDOM COME –
BLESSINGS FROM YOUR PEOPLE
ON THIS MILLENNI… UM!!

Pat Coombs, July 1999

The poem was Pat's contribution to a 'local archive thing for
2000' and was also published in a local newspaper. On sending
a corrected version to the author she would later comment:
''Course local newspaper couldn't get it quite right (!!) but
hope I've made it readable and with the right rhythm etc!'

'Furry Joys'

I've had cats – many cats… ever since I can remember
But none so dear as Frosty here
Who joined me in September

We had a Tibby – a striped old stray
The very first who came to stay.
And then a Samuel – 'Sam' for short,
A Star to follow – who knew more than he ought!

Pip I, Pip II and George came next
All friendly, furry and de-sexed!
Pip I suppsed milk with paw from jug
Pip II ditto – from an old tin mug!
All were mourned and loved and fussed
And gave us joy 'til 'Dust to Dust'.

But the one who lingers in memory clear
Is the one who lived thru' Blitz and fear
A Ginger Tom – an orphan for sure
But did we, did we shut the door?
Never! Never! Not on your life!
'Cos he was the start of our cats run rife!

Now Frosty continues this feline game
So, in pussy parlance, what's in a name?
For God be praised – they're all the same

Patty Coombs

Pat Coombs' Family Tree

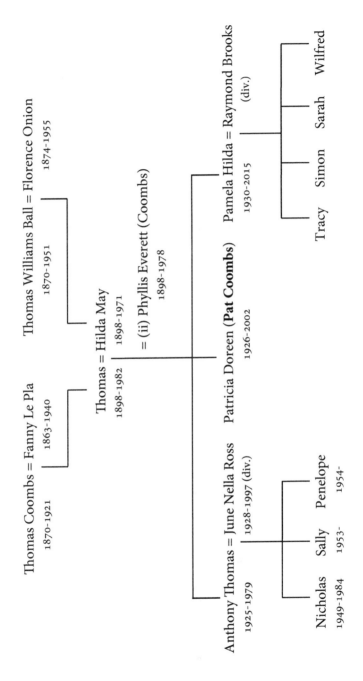

Stage credits

Include:

1947: Court Players (Scunthorpe)

1948: Little Theatre (Nottingham; plays included *When We Are Married* (as Ruby), *And No Birds Sing* (as Mrs Heron))

1949: *The Linden Tree* (as part of Harry Hanson's Court Players, Empire Theatre, Peterborough)

1953-1954: *Mother Goose* (Croydon Grand, with Cyril Fletcher, Betty Astell)

1955: *Garrison Theatre* (from Fareham, with Bob Monkhouse)

1956: *Dazzle* (Sparrow's Nest, Lowestoft, with Dick Emery)

1961: *The Summer Show of 1961* (Brighton Hippodrome, featuring Russ Conway, Alfred Marks, Freddie Mills, Janie

Marden, Ted Carson)

1976: *A Midsummer Night's A Scream* (Tiffany's, Wimbledon; charity performance with Windsor Davies, Patricia Hayes, Anna Karen, Anna Dawson, Hal Dyer, Simon Williams, Baron Rothschild)

1976-1977: *Emu's World* (pantomime with Rod Hull, Irene Handl)

1984: Charity Gala

1999: *An Evening with Pat Coombs* (charity performance, hosted by Jean Fergusson)

Film credits

1957: *A Santa for Christmas* (TV)
Director: Brian Tesler
Cast: Arthur Askey, Anthea Askey, Avril Angers.

1959: *Follow a Star* (as Simpering Girl in Theatre, uncredited)
Director: Robert Asher
Cast: Norman Wisdom, June Laverick, Jerry Desmonde,
    Hattie Jacques, John Le Mesurier, Fenella Fielding,
    Sydney Tafler, Richard Wattis.

1961: *Flying High* (TV, as WRAF)
Cast: David Lodge, William Kendall, Harry Locke, Bill Shine,
    Anna Quayle.

1962: *Maid for Murder* (aka: *She'll Have to Go*; as Lady on
    Station Platform, uncredited)
Director: Robert Asher

Cast: Bob Monkhouse, Alfred Marks, Hattie Jacques, Anna Karina, Graham Stark, Clive Dunn, Hugh Lloyd, Peter Butterworth.

1963: *A Stitch in Time* (as Nurse, uncredited)
Director: Robert Asher
Cast: Norman Wisdom, Edward Chapman, Jeanette Sterke, Jerry Desmonde, Jill Melford, Patsy Rowlands, Peter Jones.

1967: *Carry On Doctor* (as Anxious Patient, uncredited)
Director: Gerald Thomas
Cast: Sid James, Kenneth Williams, Charles Hawtrey, Joan Sims, Frankie Howerd, Jim Dale, Barbara Windsor, Hattie Jacques, Bernard Bresslaw, Anita Harris, Peter Butterworth.

1968: *Till Death Us Do Part* (as Neighbour)
Director: Norman Cohen
Cast: Warren Mitchell, Dandy Nichols, Una Stubbs, Anthony Booth, Liam Redmond, Bill Maynard, Sam Kydd, Brian Blessed, Shelagh Fraser, Ann Lancaster.

1968: *Cry Wolf* (as Mrs Blades)
Director: John Davis
Cast: Anthony Kemp, Mary Burleigh, Martin Beaumont, Judy Cornwell.

1969: *Carry On Again Doctor* (as New Matron)
Director: Gerald Thomas
Cast: Sid James, Kenneth Williams, Charles Hawtrey, Joan Sims, Hattie Jacques, Barbara Windsor, Jim Dale, Patsy Rowlands.

1970: *Plunder* (TV, as Mrs Orlock)
Cast: Tim Barrett, Megs Jenkins, Arthur Lowe, Jean Harvey,
    Richard Briers, Althea Parker.

1970: *Cucumber Castle* (TV, as Nurse Sarah Charles Bottom)
Director: Hugh Gladwish
Cast: Barry Gibb, Maurice Gibb, Eleanor Bron, Eric Clapton,
    Lulu, Frankie Howerd, Spike Milligan, Vincent Price,
    Julian Orchard.

1971: *Dad's Army* (as Mrs Hall)
Director: Norman Cohen
Cast: Arthur Lowe, John Le Mesurier, Clive Dunn, John
    Laurie, Arnold Ridley, James Beck, Ian Lavender, Frank
    Williams, Bill Pertwee, Liz Fraser.

1971: *A Couple of Beauties* (short, as Sidney's Wife)
Director: Francis Searle
Cast: Bunny Lewis, James Beck, Tim Barrett, Bernard
    Manning.

1971: *On the Buses* (as Vera)
Director: Harry Booth
Cast: Reg Varney, Doris Hare, Stephen Lewis, Anna Karen,
    Michael Robbins, Bob Grant, Andrea Lawrence, Brian
    Oulton, Wendy Richard, David Lodge.

1971: *Willy Wonka and the Chocolate Factory* (as Mrs Salt)
Director: Mel Stuart
Cast: Gene Wilder, Peter Ostrum, Jack Albertson, Roy
    Kinnear, Julie Dawn Cole, Leonard Stone, Diana Sowle.

1972: *Ooh, You Are Awful* (aka: *Get Charlie Tully*; as Libby Niven)
Director: Cliff Owen
Cast: Dick Emery, Derren Nesbitt, Ronald Fraser, William Franklyn, Cheryl Kennedy, Ambrosine Phillpotts.

1973: *Adolf Hitler – My Part in His Downfall* (as Florence Milligan, Spike's mother)
Director: Norman Cohen
Cast: Jim Dale, Spike Milligan, Arthur Lowe, Bill Maynard, Tony Selby, Geoffrey Hughes, Bob Todd, John Forgeham, Windsor Davies, Jim Norton.

1980: *High Rise Donkey* (as Lady Attending Donkey Derby)
Director: Michael Forlong
Cast: Leigh Gotch, Wendy Cook, Linda Frith, Wilfrid Brambell, Beryl Cooke, Harry Fowler, Roy Kinnear, Alfie Bass.

1984: *It's Never Too Late* (TV, as May Priggs)
Director: Graeme Muir
Cast: Peggy Mount, Hugh Lloyd, Harold Goodwin.

Television credits

Include:

1952: *Silk, Satin, Cotton, Rags* (as the Maid)

1954-55: *Fast and Loose* (4 episodes)

1955: *Garrison Theatre* *

1956: *Great Scott, It's Maynard* (8 episodes)

1956: *Val Parnell's Star Time* *

1956: *Cyril Fletcher's Roundabout* (with Cyril Fletcher, Betty Astell)

1957: *A Proper Charlie* (with Charlie Chester)

1957: *Cooper, or Life with Tommy* *

1957: *Mostly Maynard* (guest appearance)

1957: *A Santa For Christmas*

1957-58: *My Pal Bob* (7 episodes)

1957-58: *Hancock's Half Hour* (2 guest appearances as Saxon Princess & Matilda)

1958: *Saturday Spectacular – The Bob Monkhouse Hour* *

1958: *Saturday Spectacular – The David Whitfield Show* *

1958: *The Dickie Valentine Show* (with Arthur Haynes, Irene Handl, Pearl Carr, Teddy Johnson)

1959: *The Cyril Fletcher Show*

1959: *Trinder Box*

1960: *The Old Curiosity Shop*

1960: *Parade* *

1960: *Little Miss Music* *

1960: *ITV Television Playhouse – The Small Servant* (as Sophie)

1960 & 1962: *The Dickie Henderson Show* (guest appearances)

1961: *Bootsie and Snudge* (as Grace)

1961: *The Charlie Drake Show*

1961: *BBC Sunday Night Play – Wet Fish*

1962: *Six More Faces of Jim – The Face of Loyalty*

1962: *Raise Your Glasses* (with Arthur Askey)

1962: *The Tommy Steele Show: Quincy's Quest* (as Grizelda)

1963: *Comedy Bandbox* *

1963: *Comedy Playhouse – Underworld Knights* (as Café Server)

1963: *The Bing Crosby Show* (UK special with Terry-Thomas, Shirley Bassey, Dave King, Miriam Karlin)

1963, 65 & 66: *Hugh and I* (4 episodes, as Cynthia)

1964: *The Roy Castle Show* (2 guest appearances) *

1964: *The Kathy Kirby Show* *

1964: *HMS Paradise* (as Mrs Wigg)

1964: *The Arthur Haynes Show* (guest appearance)

1964: *Scott On...*

1964: *Sykes and A...*

1965: *The Roy Castle Show* (2 guest appearances, with Peter Butterworth)

1965-66: *Barney is My Darling* (4 episodes, as Miss Hobbit)

1966: *The Dick Emery Show*

1966 & 68: *Till Death Us Do Part*

1966-68: *Beggar My Neighbour* (24 episodes, as Lana Butt)

1966-80: *The Dick Emery Show* (44 episodes)

1967: *Comedy Playhouse – To Lucifer A Son*

1967: *A Series of Birds*

1968: *Ooh La La!* ('Dear Lady', as Maria)

1968: *The Jimmy Logan Show* (BBC Show of the Week) *

1969: *Mr Digby Darling* (as Dulcie)

1969: *Comedy Playhouse – The Making of Peregrine* (as Minerva Mold)

1969: *Wild, Wild Women* (series, 6 episodes, as Daisy)

1969: *The Jimmy Logan Show* *

1969: *Galton and Simpson Comedy – Don't Dilly Dally on the Way* (as Joyce Croucher)

1969: *Dombey and Son* (5 episodes, as Lucretia Tox)

1969: *Going for a Song*

1969: *The Dick Emery Show*

1970: *Sandler and Young's Kraft Music Hall* *

1970: *Up Pompeii!* ('The Legacy', as Tarta the Sorceress)

1970: *Here Come the Double Deckers!* (2 episodes, as Doris Fisher)

1970: *This Is Your Life* (Reg Varney) *

1970: *Crowther's Back In Town* (with Irene Handl) *

1970: *Playschool* (storyteller) *

1970: *Comedy Playhouse – Meter Maids* (as Crocker)

1971: *Mr Digby Darling* (as Ida)

1971: *The Dick Emery Show* (4 episodes)

1971-72: *Lollipop* (as Violet)

1972: *Cranford* (4 episodes, as Miss Pole)

1972: *The Reg Varney Revue* (4 episodes and Christmas Special)

1972-73: *The Dick Emery Show* (2 series, 13 episodes)

1973: *The Best of Dick Emery*

1973: *Son of the Bride* (2 guest appearances, as Mrs Beadle)

1973: *Sykes* ('Uniform', as bus conductress)

1974: *The Reg Varney Show* (145 episodes)

1974-75: *Don't Drink the Water* (as Dorothy Blake)

1974-75: *Till Death Us Do Part* (4 guest appearances, as Neighbour/Mrs Carey)

1974-75: *The Dick Emery Show* (8 episodes)

1974: *The Dick Emery Christmas Show*

1975: *Jackanory Playhouse* ('The Queen and the Robot', as Lady Cynthia)

1976: *Hogg's Back* (series, as Mrs Mac)

1976: *James and the Giant Peach* (as Miss Spider)

1976: *Nobody Does It Like Marti* *

1976: *The Queen and the Robot* (as Lady Cynthia)

1976: *The Dick Emery Show*

1976 & 78: *Those Wonderful Times* (interview) *

1977: *The Dick Emery Show*

1977 & 1979: *The Basil Brush Show* (guest appearances)

1978: *Golden Gala* *

1978: *Star Turn* (2 guest appearances) *

1978 & 79: *3-2-1* *

1978-81: *You're Only Young Twice* (31 episodes, as Cissie Lupin)

1978: *Have A Harry Birthday* (Harry Secombe *Alice in Wonderland* birthday special)

1979, 80, 81, 82, 83, 84, 85, 87 & 89: *Blankety Blank* (guest appearances in 11 episodes) *

1980: *The Dick Emery Show* (2 episodes)

1980: *We'll Tell You A Story* *

1980: *Speak for Yourself* (as Shop Assistant)

1980: *Keep it in the Family* ('All Through the Night', as Miss Petty)

1981, 83 & 84: *Punchlines* (7 episodes) *

1981: *Now for Nookie* (with Nicholas Smith, David Lodge)

1981: *Look Who's Talking* *

1981: *Playschool – The Queen Who Couldn't Sleep* *

1982: *Ragdolly Anna* (series, 6 episodes, as the Dressmaker/Narrator)

1982: *Whose Baby?* *

1982: *The Pyramid Game* *

1982: *The Jim Davidson Show* *

1982: *This Is Your Life* (Diana Dors) *

1983: *Make Me Laugh*

1983-84: *Lady is a Tramp* (2 series, 13 episodes, as Lanky Pat)

1984: *The Marti Caine Show*

1984: *Mooncat & Co.* (guest appearances, billed as Pat Coombes)

1984-85: *The Zodiac Game* (guest appearances) *

1985: *Supergran* ('Supergran and the Raid on Race Day', as Miss Wotherspoon)

1985: *Masterpiece Theatre: Bleak House* (as Mrs Guppy)

1985: *Rainbow* ('Books – The Library', as Patty)

1985: *Child's Play* *

1985-87: *Ragdolly Anna* (2 series, 24 episodes, as the Dressmaker/Narrator)

1986: *All Star Secrets* (with Barbara Windsor, Michael Barrymore, Jeffrey Holland, Ronnie Scott) *

1986: *Emu's All Live Pink Windmill Show* (as Witch Curdle)

1987: *Supergran* ('Supergran and the Heir Apparent', as Miz Witherspoon)

1987: *Emu's World* (3 episodes, as Lady Petunia)

1987: *3-2-1 Christmas Special* *

1987: *Playbox* – 'Birds' (as the voice of the Cat)

1987: *Wogan* (Wogan's Radio Fun) *

1988: *An Audience with Victoria Wood* *

1988: *Wogan* (Bob Monkhouse 60th birthday special) *

1988-89: *Mr Majeika* (3 episodes, as Miss Flavia Jelly)

1989: *The Joke Machine* *

1989: *Pob's Programme* (guest appearance) *

1989-90: *EastEnders* (59 episodes, as 'Brown Owl' Marge Green)

1990: *The Krypton Factor* ('Observation' segment, as Arbuthnot)

1990: *Krankies Television*

1990-92: *In Sickness and in Health* (9 episodes, as Mrs Carey)

1991: *Roy's Raiders*

1991: *An Actor's Life For Me* ('Fathers and Sons', as Mrs Dobbs)

1992: *Birds of a Feather* ('Breadwinner', as Gloria)

1992: *Boon* ('The Sharp End', as Doris)

1992: *Wogan* (with Peggy Mount) *

1992-95: *Noel's House Party* (guest appearances, as Prudence 'Pru' Prendergast)

1993: *Celebrity Squares* (2 episodes) *

1993: *Telly Addicts* (with Richard O'Sullivan) *

1994: *An Audience with Ken Dodd* *

1994: *An Audience with Bob Monkhouse* *

1995: *That's Showbusiness* (with Mike Smith, Phill Jupitus) *

1995: *This Is Your Life* (June Whitfield) *

1996: *Valentine*

1997: *Dick Emery: A Life on the Box* *

1997: *This Is Your Life* (Graham Cole)*

2000: *Treasure* (voice only)

2000: *Barrymore* (guest) *

2001: *Doctors* ('A Wonderful Life', as Irene Morris)

2002: *Dick Emery – Heroes of Comedy* *

* as herself

Radio credits

Include:

1949: *Here's Howard* (with Michael Howard)

1954-55: *Hello Playmates* (with Arthur Askey)

1955: *Garrison Theatre*

1955: *Hello, Blackpool Playmates!*

1955: *The Man About Town*

1955: *Starstruck* (with Bob Monkhouse, Denis Goodwin)

1955: *Hello, Christmas Playmates!* (as The Mince Pie, featuring Petula Clark)

1955: *Bring on the Girls* (as Nola, with Irene Handl, June Whitfield)

1955: *Nixon Mix* (with Irene Handl)

1956-57: *Mixed Doubles* (with Cyril Fletcher)

1956: *Midday Music Hall* (with Irene Handl)

1956-57 & 59-60, 61: *Ray's a Laugh* (with Ted Ray)

1956: *Bank Holiday Matinee* (with Irene Handl)

1957: *Easter Bandbox* (with Irene Handl)

1957: *A Proper Charlie* (with Charlie Chester)

1958 & 59: *London Lights* (with Irene Handl)

1958: *The Arthur Askey Show*

1958: *Dick Whittington* (Christmas Special, as Marilyn, with Arthur Askey, Richard Murdoch, Kenneth Connor, Shani Wallis)

1959: *That Man Chester* (with Charlie Chester)

1960: *Frankie's Bandbox* (with Frankie Howerd, Alma Cogan)

1960: *Midday Music Hall* (with Irene Handl)

1960: *Cyril Fletcher's Holiday Music-Hall* (with Irene Handl)

1960: *Leave it to the Boys*

1960: *Law and Disorder* (as Betty Bilston)

1961: *London Lights* (guest appearances, with Ronnie Barker, Hugh Paddick)

1962: *Monday Night at Home* (with Peter Jones)

1962: *The Men from the Ministry*

1962: *Show Time*

1963: *Dishonest to Goodness* (series, with Bernard Bresslaw)

1963: *Star Parade*

1963: *Variety Playhouse*

1964: *How's Your Father?* (with Ted Ray, Thora Hird, Terence Alexander)

1964: *Star's Choice* (with Irene Handl)

1964: *Comedy Parade: The Don Arrol Programme*

1964: *Music-Hall* (with Irene Handl)

1965: *Star Time* (with Irene Handl)

1965: *Home and Away* (with Irene Handl)

1965: *Sid and Dora* (with Sid James, Dora Byan)

1965: *Light up the Night* (with Irene Handl)

1965: *The Arthur Haynes Show*

1965: *This Is Your Jim* (with Jimmy Edwards)

1967: *Harry Worth* (with James Beck)

1970: *Seekers* (with Prunella Scales)

1970-72: *The Ken Dodd Show*

1971: *Don't Forget Me in Mine, Mum*

1971: *Life Is What You Make It* (with Michael Robbins)

1972: *Steptoe and Son* (with Patricia Hayes)

1972 & 74: *Sounds Familiar*

1973: *Christmas Morning*

1973: *The Things* (with Michael Robbins)

1974: *Wogan's World*

1975: *Celebration*

1975: *The Men from the Ministry*

1975: *Dad's Army* ('A Soldier's Farewell', The Clippie/Marie)

1975: *I'm Ken, He's Bill*

1976: *Funny You Should Ask* (panellist)

1976: *It's All in the Mind of David Morgan* (panellist)

1976: *Ode to Cyril Fletcher*

1976: *Does the Team Think?*

1977: *Pros and Cons* (panellist)

1977-79: *Albert and Me* (with Richard Beckinsale, John Comer)

1978: *Thank You Mrs Fothergill* (with Sheila Hancock, Avis Bunnage)

1979: *My Sainted Aunt* (with Trevor Bannister, Eleanor Summerfield)

1980: *Sailor, Beware!* (with Peggy Mount)

1980: *Oh Mother!* (with Mollie Sugden)

1981: *Speak for Yourself*

1981 & 83: *Know Your Place* (with Roy Dotrice, Patricia Hayes and later with Sheila Hancock)

1983: *Kenneth Williams Cabaret* (with Julie Covington)

1985, 86, 87: *Some of These Days* (panellist)

1985: *Castle's Corner* (with Roy Castle, special guest)

1986: *The Press Gang* (panellist)

1986: *The Christmas Jottings of Hinge and Bracket* (guest, with Deryck Guyler)

1987: *The Law Game* (panellist)

1987: *You and Me* (as Mrs Blades)

1988: *Inman and Friends*

1988: *The Pilgrim's Postscript*

1990: *Mind Your Own Business!* (series, as Ethel, with Bernard Cribbins, Kenneth Connor)

1992-95: *Queen of Romance* (with Lesley Joseph)

1993: *Starting Out with Terry*

1994: *A Perfect Spy* (as Daisy)

1996: *Late Night Opening – Educated Evans* (with Roy Hudd, Andrew Sachs)

1996: *The Monday Play: The L-Shaped Room* (as Mrs Blades)

1997: *King Street Junior* (as Betty Austin)

1998: *Babblewick Hall* (with Elizabeth Spriggs)

1998-2002: *Like They've Never Been Gone* (4 series, as Hetty)

1999: *Schools Radio* (with Roy Hudd)

Bibliography

Crawford, Kaye, *Roll Out the Beryl! The Authorised Biography of Beryl Reid*, Fantom Publishing, 2016.

Cornwell, Judy, *Adventures of a Jelly Baby,* Sidgwick & Jackson, 2005.

Davies, Russell (editor), *The Kenneth Williams Diaries*, HarperCollins Publishers, 1993.

Hayward, Anthony, *Who's Who on Television*, Boxtree, 1990 & 1996.

Hodgson, Michael, *Anthony Steel – The Wooden Dish*, New Generation Publishing, 2016.

Kenward, Jean, *Ragdolly Anna*, Puffin Books, 1979.

Lewisohn, Mark, *Radio Times Guide to TV Comedy*, BBC Worldwide, 1998.

Lloyd, Hugh, *Thank God For A Funny Face*, John Blake, 2002.

Perry, Jimmy, *A Stupid Boy*, Century, 2002.

Ridley, Nicholas, *Godfrey's Ghost – From Father to Son*, Mogzilla Life, 2009.

Ross, Andrew, *Everything I Ever Wanted – The Life and Career of Peggy Mount*, Fantom Publishing, 2019.

Stevens, Christopher, *Born Brilliant – The Life of Kenneth Williams*, John Murray (Publishers), 2010.

Stone, Richard, *You Should Have Been in Last Night*, The Book Guild Limited, 2000.

Whitfield, June, *… And June Whitfield*, Bantam Press, 2000.

Notes on the chapters

Chapter 1: Pomegranates and oranges

1. *Woman's Weekly*, 1989
2. Thomas William Coombs, born 10th October 1898, Camberwell, Surrey
3. *Woman's Weekly*, 1989
4. *Woman's Weekly*, 1989
5. Penny Hey, email to the author, 2019
6. *Woman's Weekly*, 1989. Built by J. McManus Ltd, it was opened on Empire Day, 24th May 1917, by various dignitaries including the Countess of Lansborough, the Countess of Wilton and the Mayor of Camberwell, Thomas Coombs. Run by a Miss Marjorie Butter, the hut had a billiard room, reading rooms and 150 beds for those staying overnight. Many injured troops from a nearby military hospital would visit the hut to attend concerts and use its facilities. The hut was visited by the Queen of Romania, Queen Victoria's granddaughter, during one of her visits to London. https://www.southwarknews.co.uk/history/the-wwi-hut-that-camberwell-built/
7. *Woman's Weekly*, 1989
8. *Woman's Weekly*, 1989

9 *The Guardian*, 28th May 2002

10 *Woman's Weekly*, 1989

11 'Patty's Pome' (see Appendix) revealed her dislike of the school

12 *TV Times*, 3rd August 1972

13 *Daily Mirror*, 2nd September 1978

14 *TV Times*, 3rd August 1972

15 *My Weekly*, 21st October 1972

16 Irene Sutcliffe played Maggie Clegg/Cooke in more than 400 episodes of *Coronation Street* from 1968-74/75. The character was the younger sister of Betty Turpin/Williams (played by Betty Driver) and the adopted mother of Gordon (played by Bill Kenwright). Irene continued to act on television until 2015, and from 2000 was a vice-president of the Actors' Benevolent Fund. She died in May 2019, aged ninety-four, leaving an estate valued at more than £1.3million.

17 *The Telegraph*, 15th October 1992

18 Unnamed newspaper interview, 1969, Pat Coombs archive/estate

19 *My Weekly*, 21st October 1972

20 *TV Times*, 3rd August 1972

21 *TV Times*, 3rd August 1972

22 *Radio Times*, 27th May-7th June 1989

23 *TV Times*, 3rd August 1972

24 Pat is also credited with playing 'the sinister Mrs Danvers in Daphne du Maurier's *Rebecca*' but I have been unable to verify this appearance; *TV Times*, 5-11th August 1972.

25 *TV Times*, 3rd August 1972

26 *The Independent*, 10th June 2002

27 *Daily Mirror*, 2nd September 1978

28 Unnamed newspaper interview, 1969, Pat Coombs archive/estate

29 *My Weekly*, 21st October 1972

30 *My Weekly*, 21st October 1972

31 Unnamed newspaper interview, 1969, Pat Coombs archive/estate

Chapter 2: 'Speak as you find, that's my motto'

1 Elizabeth Monkhouse was the daughter of former Irish football international Tommy Thompson. She married Bob Monkhouse in 1949

and they had three children: Gary (who died from cerebral palsy in 1992 aged forty), Simon (who died from a heroin overdose in Thailand in 2001) and Abigail. The couple divorced in 1972.

2 Gale Pedrick's column, Spring 1958

3 Gale Pedrick's column, Spring 1958

4 Dabber Davis, interview with the author, 2020. Denis Goodwin died from an overdose of sleeping tablets on 26th February 1975, aged forty-five.

5 *Radio Times*, 10th December 1954

6 *Sheffield Star*, 23rd March 1955

7 *Sheffield Star*, 23rd March 1955

8 Pat Coombs, letter to the author, 7th December 1999

9 Pat Coombs, letter to the author, 7th December 1999

10 Dabber Davis, interview with the author, 2020

11 *My Weekly*, 21st October 1972

12 *The Stage*, 26th July 1956

13 *Yorkshire Evening Post*, 10th June 1989

14 Gale Pedrick's column, Spring 1958

15 Judy Cornwell, *Adventures of a Jelly Baby*, p. 165

16 Undated newspaper article, Pat Coombs archive/estate

Chapter 3: Mool and Moolie

1 *Beckham and Penge Advertiser*, 13th December 1951

2 *The Times*, 3rd August 1972

3 *Titbits*, 27th May 1976

4 *Reveille*, 15th-22nd July 1972

5 *Titbits*, 27th May 1976

6 *Radio Times*, 27th May-2nd June 1989

7 *Yorkshire Evening Post*, 10th June 1989

8 *Sunday Mirror*, 1st September 1974

9 *Radio Times*, 27th May-2nd June 1989

10 Pam Valentine, interview with the author, 2020

11 *Radio Times*, 27th May-2nd June 1989

12 *TV Times*, 3rd August 1972

[13] A reference to a storyline in *EastEnders*, in which Pat was appearing at the time.

[14] Pat Coombs archive

[15] Lisa Blunt, letter to the author, 2020

[16] *The Stage*, 19th October 1995

[17] *The Stage*, 21st September 1995

[18] George Raistrick, Last Will & Testament, Probate Records, In the High Court of Justice, The District Probate Registry at Birmingham, 5th December 1995

[19] *Reveille*, 15th-22nd July 1972

[20] *Titbits*, 27th May 1976

[21] *Daily Mail*, 20th September 1978

[22] Pat Coombs scrapbook, c. 1972

[23] *Titbits*, 27th May 1976

[24] *Titbits*, 27th May 1976

[25] *Liverpool Echo*, 10th September 1977

[26] *Titbits*, 27th May 1976

[27] Sue Sinclair, email to the author, 2019

[28] *Heroes of Comedy*: 'Dick Emery', documentary, 2002

[29] *Daily Mail*, 6th March 2001

[30] *Heroes of Comedy*: 'Dick Emery', documentary, 2002

[31] *Titbits*, 27th May 1976

[32] *Echo Extra*, 1972

[33] *Daily Telegraph*, 28th May 2002

[34] Pat Coombs, letter to the author, 29th February 2000

Chapter 4: 'Gravy-ating'

[1] *The Times Education Supplement*, 22nd January 1960

[2] *TV Times*, 5-11th August 1972

[3] *TV Times*, 5-11th August 1972

[4] *The People*, 19th March 1967

[5] In her autobiography June Whitfield would write: 'Patti and I go back a long way. I think we first worked together on a Forces radio show called *Bring on the Girls* some time in the Fifties.' ... *And June Whitfield*, 2000.

[6] *Echo Extra*, undated, 1972

[7] *My Weekly*, 21st October 1972

[8] Mike Sharland, email to the author, 2020

[9] *Echo Extra*, undated, 1972

[10] Pam Valentine would confirm 'it's every actor's paranoia that they'll never work again and many actors watch every penny because of this'; interview with the author, 2020.

[11] Eleanor Bron, letter to the author, 2020

[12] Jacki Piper, email to the author, 2019

[13] *The Stage and Television Today*, 22nd May 1969

[14] *Radio Times Guide to TV Comedy*

[15] In *Meter Maids* Pat was reunited with Barbara Windsor and Joan Sanderson, who had also starred in *Wild Wild Women*. Despite the stellar cast which also included Queenie Watts, Martin Wyldeck and Bob Todd the idea was not commissioned into a series.

[16] *The Stage and Television Today*, 21st August 1969

[17] Sally Cryer, email to the author, 2020

[18] Simon Brooks, email to the author, 2020

Chapter 5: A stalwart stooge

[1] For her work in PG Tips television commercials Pat was required to work with a number of chimpanzees, including Louis, a chimpanzee that died at Twycross Zoo in 2013, aged thirty-seven. They were photographed together in 1982.

[2] Tracy Lynch, email to the author, 2019

[3] Another notable piece of commercial work for Pat was an advert for Woolworths along with seventeen other stars including Nicholas Parsons, Anita Harris, Leslie Crowther, Windsor Davies and Tim Brooke-Taylor.

[4] *Leicester Mercury*, undated c.1974. The record would appear in the 1979 edition of *The Guinness Book of Records*.

[5] Pat Coombs, letter to the author, 16th May 2000

[6] *The Stage*, 8th December 2008

[7] Pat Coombs, letter to the author, 14th May 1997

[8] *My Weekly*, 21st October 1972

[9] In which Mount, Lloyd and Pat would later star; see Chapter 7.

[10] Ian Masters, interview with the author, 2017

[11] Jimmy Perry, *A Stupid Boy*

[12] Hugh Lloyd, *Thank God For A Funny Face*

[13] Hilda Coombs died at the King Edward VII Memorial Hospital, Haywards Heath, on 20th December 1971, aged seventy-three. The cause of death was attributed to coronary thrombosis and hypertension.

[14] Penny Hey, email to the author, 2020

[15] Penny Hey, email to the author, 2020

[16] *Reveille*, 15th-22nd July 1972

[17] *Titbits*, 27th May 1976

[18] Thomas Coombs married Phyllis Everett on 21st October 1972

[19] *TV Times*, 3rd August 1972

[20] *TV Times*, 3rd August 1972

[21] Penny Hey, email to the author, 2020

[22] Penny Hey, email to the author, 2020

[23] *Radio Times*, 27th May-7th June 1989

[24] *TV Times*, 3rd August 1972

[25] Georgina Moon, interview with the author, 2019

[26] Pam Valentine, interview with the author, 2020

[27] Dabber Davis, interview with the author, 2020

[28] Penny Hey, email to the author, 2020

[29] In the 1950s she was frequently photographed in her bathing costume – although she never swam and didn't particularly like the water.

[30] Undated newspaper article, c. 1975, Pat Coombs archive/estate

[31] *My Weekly*, 21st October 1972

[32] *Liverpool Echo*, 10th September 1977

[33] Undated article, c. 1972, Pat Coombs archive/estate

[34] Penny Hey, email to the author, 2020

[35] Richard Stone, *You Should Have Been in Last Night*

[36] *Liverpool Echo*, 10th September 1977

[37] Penny Hey, email to the author, 2019

[38] *Midweek Observer and Gazette*, 3rd August 1971

[39] Anne's second husband would predecease her after collapsing and dying in their garden. In Pat's will Anne was bequeathed £30,000, along with Pat's 'Adjustomatic orthopaedic bed and small oak bookcase'. Following

Pat's death, Anne moved to Ireland where she lived until her death in 2014.

[40] Penny Hey, email to the author, 2020

[41] Pat Coombs, note to Penny Hey, 1993, Pat Coombs archive/estate

[42] Simon Brooks, email to the author, 2020

[43] *My Weekly*, 21st October 1972

[44] *TV Times*, 3rd August 1972

[45] Steve Doherty, interview with the author, 2020

[46] Simon Brooks, email to the author, 2020

[47] *Pinner Observer*, 21st October 1999

[48] *Daily Mirror*, 29th December 1972

[49] Letter from Dr Laurance Barclay to Pat Coombs, 28th December 1972, Pat Coombs archive/estate

[50] *Newcastle Evening Chronicle*, 30th December 1972

[51] *Newcastle Evening Chronicle*, 30th December 1972

[52] Dabber Davis, interview with the author, 2020

[53] Simon Brooks, email to the author, 2020

[54] *TV Times*, 3rd August 1972

[55] Undated article, Pat Coombs archive/estate

[56] Derek Griffiths, letter to the author, 2019

[57] *Radio Times Guide to TV Comedy*

[58] Amazingly, for a variety of reasons, the film was never publicly seen until 2018.

[59] *TV Times*, 1976

[60] *The Stage*, 21st October 1976

[61] Pat Coombs, letters to the author, 7th December 1999 and 15th January 2000

[62] *Titbits*, May 1976

[63] Chris Emmett, email to the author, 18th August 2019

[64] *Sunday People*, 23rd November 1975

[65] *Sunday People*, 23rd November 1975

[66] *Daily Mirror*, 2nd September 1978

[67] Pat Morris, email to the author, 2020

[68] Kate Lock, letter to the author, 25th September 2019

[69] Jim Eldridge, email to the author, 2020

Chapter 6: A lifetime of comedy

1   *Sunday Mirror*, 20th September 1977
2   *Evening Post*, 6th September 1977
3   Pam Valentine, interview with the author, 2020. Pam Valentine and Michael Ashton first met at a parent-teacher association meeting in Cheltenham where they both had children at the same school. A stage playwright, Michael had no television experience but at that stage had already written a lot for the theatre. Pam's career had already included writing sketches for *The Two Ronnies*, and later the pair would work together on thirty-five episodes of *That's My Boy* and seven episodes of *My Husband and I* (both starring Mollie Sugden).
4   *Evening Express*, 27th September 1977
5   *Evening Post*, 6th September 1977
6   *Wogan*, 1992.
7   Georgina Moon, interview with the author, 2019
8   Georgina Moon, interview with the author, 2016
9   John Standing, interview with the author, 2017
10 Pam Valentine, interview with the author, 2020
11 Pam Valentine, interview with the author, 2017
12 Pam Valentine, interview with the author, 2020
13 *East Kent Mercury*, 16th February 1978
14 Pam Valentine, interview with the author, 2017
15 Pam Valentine, interview with the author, 2020
16 Pam Valentine, interview with the author, 2017
17 *Daily Mirror*, 14th June 1979
18 Johnnie Wade, email to the author, 2017
19 *The Stage*, 7th June 2002
20 Pam Valentine, interview with the author 2019
21 Pam Valentine, interview with the author, 2020
22 *The Sun*, 2nd January 1990
23 *Liverpool Echo*, 10th September 1977
24 *Sunday Mirror*, 20th September 1977
25 *Sunday Mirror*, 20th September 1977
26 *Daily Mirror*, 22nd October 1977
27 Simon Brooks, email to the author, 2020

[28] Pat Coombs, letter to the author, 8th August 1999

[29] Penny Hey, email to the author, 2019

[30] *Woman's Weekly*, 1989

[31] Private letter from Pat Coombs archive/estate

[32] Thomas Coombs, 6th January 1898-17th May 1982

[33] *Evening News and Star*, 20th July 1981

[34] Pat Coombs, letter to the author, 28th October 1999

[35] Pat Coombs, letter to the author, 5th November 2000

Chapter 7: Changing times

[1] *The Independent*, 1st October 1993

[2] Damaris Hayman, interview with the author, 7th September 2015. Hayman and Griffiths shared a mutual friend, Dame Margaret Rutherford, who was well known for her financial generosity to less well-off actors.

[3] *Daily Mirror*, 2nd September 1978

[4] *Radio Times*, 27th May-7th June 1989

[5] Georgina Moon, interview with the author, 2019

[6] Robert Gillespie, Twitter, 28th January 2020

[7] Dame Sheila Hancock DBE, letter to the author, November 2019

[8] *The Sun*, 4th September 1976

[9] Pat also featured in the film version of *Till Death Us Do Part* playing a neighbour.

[10] *The Sun*, 4th September 1976

[11] *Radio Times Guide to TV Comedy*

[12] *Daily Mail*, 18th February 1984

[13] Pam Valentine, interview with the author, 2020

[14] *Daily Star*, 13th April 1984

[15] *Evening News and Star*, 20th July 1981

[16] Ian Masters, interview with the author, 2020

[17] *News of the World*, 27th May 1984

[18] *Sunday People*, 27th May 1984

[19] Penny Hey, email to the author, 2020

[20] *Australian Telegraph*, 18th December 1983

[21] *Australian Telegraph*, 18th December 1983

[22] *People Magazine*, 19th September 1983

[23] *People Magazine*, 19th September 1983

[24] Private letter, Pat Coombs archive/estate

[25] Pat had previously worked with Roger seven years earlier in his 1981 television series, and in 2020 he would remember her as 'a delightful actress and a pleasure to work with'. (Roger de Courcey, email to the author, 2020)

[26] Jean Kenward, *Ragdolly Anna*. In the series the Little Dressmaker lived on the third floor of a block of flats, with the exterior shots being filmed at Woolman Street, Marsh Lane, in Leeds. The flats were originally built in 1908 to rehouse tenants of slum properties in the nearby area. They have since been demolished.

[27] *South Wales Evening Post*, 6th April 1987

[28] Caroline Berry, Twitter to the author, 2020

[29] Caroline Berry, Twitter to the author, 2020

[30] Jean Kenward, *Ragdolly Anna*

[31] Georgia Ross, email to the author, 2020

[32] Jean Kenward, letter to the author, July 2020

[33] Allan Taylor, email to the author, 2020

[34] Anne Wood CBE, interview with the author, 2019

[35] *The Stage*, 9th January 2003

[36] *The Stage*, 9th January 2003

[37] *Evening Herald*, Dublin, 8th December 1987

[38] Pat Coombs, letter to the author, 7th December 1999

Chapter 8: *EastEnders*

[1] *South London Press*, 23rd June 1989

[2] Simon Brooks, email to the author, 2020

[3] Barry Burnett, interview with the author, 2019

[4] Barry Burnett, interview with the author, 2019

[5] *The Sun*, 17th May 1989

[6] *Radio Times*, 27th May-7th June 1989

[7] *Daily Star*, 3rd May 1989

[8] *Yorkshire Evening Post*, 10th June 1989

[9] Letter from Barbara Knox MBE to Pat Coombs, Pat Coombs archive/estate

[10] *Yorkshire Evening Post*, 10th June 1989

[11] *South London Press*, 23rd June 1989

[12] *Yorkshire Evening Post*, 10th June 1989. Although Marge was a spinster, Pat was permitted by *EastEnders'* producers to continue wearing her mother's old wedding ring and the engagement ring given to her in 1951. 'Viewers will probably be puzzled,' admitted Pat, although it never seemed to attract attention.

[13] *Yorkshire Evening Post*, 10th June 1989

[14] *Daily Mirror*, 28th November 1989

[15] *Daily Mail*, 6th March 1990

[16] *South London Press*, 23rd June 1989

[17] Christmas card from Barbara Knox MBE to Pat Coombs, Pat Coombs archive

[18] Letter from Michael Ferguson, 22nd December 1989, Pat Coombs archive/estate

[19] *The Sun*, 2nd January 1990

[20] *The Sun*, 2nd January 1990

[21] *The Sun*, 2nd January 1990

[22] *The Sun*, 2nd January 1990

[23] *The Sun*, 28th December 1989

[24] Wincey Willis, letter to Pat Coombs, 15th June 1989, Pat Coombs archive/estate

[25] *The Sun*, 2nd January 1990

[26] *The Sun*, 6th March 1991. It is interesting to note that of the mentioned actors many did continue working until the very end of their lives. Joan Sanderson filmed two television series, *After Henry* and *Land of Hope and Gloria* shortly before her death in 1992, Eric Sykes continued to work as an actor until the age of eighty-seven, and Pat Coombs was still working on radio and appeared on television just months before her death in 2002.

[27] *The Sun*, 6th November 1990

[28] Paul Mayhew-Archer, email to the author, 2019

[29] *TV Weekly*, 12-18th September 1992

[30] Pat Coombs, letter to the author, 28th October 1999

[31] Gary Lawson, interview with the author, 2020

[32] Pat Coombs, letter to Penny Hey, 21st May 1993

[33] *Welwyn and Hatfield Comet Weekender*, 26th March 1993

[34] Graham Cole OBE, email to the author, 2020

[35] *Sunday Express*, 29th August 1993

[36] Georgia Ross, email to the author, 2020

[37] *Welwyn and Hatfield Comet Weekender*, 26th March 1993

[38] Jim Eldridge, email to the author, 2020

Chapter 9: Battling on

[1] Pat Coombs, letter to the author, 15th January 1998

[2] *Daily Mail*, 22nd April 1997

[3] *Daily Mail*, 22nd April 1997

[4] Penny Hey, interview with the author, 2020

[5] *Daily Mail*, 26th January 1996

[6] Helen Kingman, email to the author, 2020

[7] *Daily Mail*, 22nd April 1997

[8] Pat Coombs, letter to the author, 14th May 1997

[9] Pat Coombs, letter to the author, 14th May 1997

Chapter 10: To Denville

[1] *The Stage*, 17th May 2001

[2] Mike Coleman, email to the author, 2020

[3] Steve Doherty, email and interview with the author, 2020

[4] Pat Coombs, letter to the author, 1st September 1998

[5] Pat Coombs, letter to the author, 1st September 1998

[6] Pat Coombs, letter to the author, 1st September 1998

[7] Pat Coombs, letter to the author, 5th December 1998

[8] Pat Coombs, letter to the author, 16th February 1999

[9] Pat Coombs, letter to the author, 12th April 1999

[10] Pat Coombs, letter to the author, 15th May 1999

[11] Pat Coombs, letter to the author, 26th May 1999

[12] Pat Coombs, letter to the author, 26th June 1999

[13] Pat Coombs, letter to the author, 26th June 1999

[14] *The Independent*

[15] Ian Talbot, interview with the author, 2017

[16] Mark Curry, email to the author, 2018

[17] Jeffrey Holland, interview with the author, 2017

[18] Gillian Bryant, email to the author, 2020

[19] Eira Griffiths, interview with the author, 2017

[20] Pat Coombs, letter to the author, 28th October 1999

[21] Pat Coombs, letter to the author, 28th September 1999

[22] Pat Coombs, letter to the author, 28th September 1999

[23] Pat Coombs, letter to the author, 28th October 1999

[24] Pat Coombs, letter to the author, 7th December 1999

[25] Pat Coombs, letter to the author, 15th January 2000

[26] Pat Coombs, letter to the author, 15th January 2000

[27] Pat Coombs, letter to the author, 6th March 1997

[28] Pat Coombs, letter to the author, 15th January 2000. Arnold Ridley had lived at Denville Hall at the very end of his life before dying in hospital in March 1984 following a fall. His widow, the actress Althea Parker, to whom he was married from 1945 until his death, lived at Denville until her death in February 2001.

[29] Pat Coombs, letter to the author, 15th January 2000

[30] *Choice*, June 2000

[31] Pat would update her car regularly, a rare extravagance, but despite being a tall lady for most of her life, she always bought very small, economical vehicles.

[32] Pat Coombs, letter to the author, 16th May 2000

[33] Pat Coombs, letter to the author, 28th July 2000

[34] Pam Valentine, interview with the author, 2020

[35] Pat Coombs, letter to the author, 16th August 2000

[36] Pat Coombs, letter to the author, 3rd September 2000

[37] Pat Coombs, letter to the author, 5th November 2000

[38] Pat Coombs, letter to the author, 5th April 2000

[39] Pat Coombs, letter to the author, 16th May 2000

[40] Pat Coombs, letter to the author, 3rd September 2000

[41] Chris Emmett, email to the author, 2019

[42] Pat Coombs, letter to the author, 3rd September 2000

[43] Michael Hodgson, *Anthony Steel – The Wooden Dish*, p. 246

[44] Pat Coombs, letter to the author, 3rd September 2000

[45] Pat Coombs, letter to the author, 5th October 2000

[46] Michael Hodgson, *Anthony Steel – The Wooden Dish*

[47] Conversation with Penny Hey, 2020

[48] Pat Coombs, letter to the author, 5th November 2000

[49] Pam Valentine, interview with the author, 2020

[50] Anne Wood CBE, interview with the author, 2019

[51] Steve Doherty, interview with the author, 2020

[52] Pat Coombs, letter to the author, 16th May 2000

[53] Lisa Bowerman, email to the author, 2020

[54] Pat Coombs, letter to the author, 5th October 2000

[55] Sue Sinclair, email to the author, 2019

[56] Pat Coombs, letter to the author, 5th December 2000

[57] Pat Coombs, letter to the author, 5th November 2000

[58] Pat Coombs, letter to the author, 5th November 2000

[59] Lord Attenborough died at Denville Hall on 24th August 2014 at the age of ninety. His wife, who spent the last six years of her life at Denville battling dementia, died on 19th January 2016, aged ninety-three.

[60] Anne Wood CBE, interview with the author, 2019

[61] Gary Lawson, interview with the author, 2020

[62] Pat Coombs, letter to the author, 18th April 2001

[63] Zulema Dene, letter to the author, 2017

[64] *Daily Mail*, 22nd April 1997

[65] *Yours*, February 2002

[66] Steve Doherty, interview with the author, 2020

[67] *The Independent*, 10th June 2002

[68] *The Independent*, 10th June 2002

[69] It was later reported in the press and on the internet that Pat was suffering from gangrene and had refused a life-extending operation which would have involved amputation. Her death certificate listed the official causes as peripheral vascular disease (an untreatable condition leading to muscle pain, weakness and numbness) and chronic obstructive airways disease. Both conditions could be directly linked to Pat's lifelong smoking habit.

[70] *Daily Telegraph*, 28th May 2002

71 *The Sun*, 28th May 2002

72 *Daily Mirror*, 28th May 2002

73 *Daily Mirror*, 28th May 2002

74 *The Sun*, 28th May 2002

75 *The Sun*, 28th May 2002

76 *Daily Mirror*, 28th May 2002

77 bbc.co.uk

78 *Harrow Observer*, 28th May 2002

79 Pat Morris, email to the author, 2020

80 Chris Emmett, email to the author, 2019

81 Steve Doherty, email to the author, 2020

82 *Harrow Observer*, 7th June 2002

83 *Harrow Observer*, 7th June 2002

84 *Harrow Observer*, 7th June 2002

85 Leo Marks, *The Life That I Have*, Souvenir Press, 1999

86 Pat's flat had flooded in the autumn of 2000, just months after she had moved into Denville Hall. She would write: 'No. 5 Wendela has had an unbelievable catastrophe – flooded!!! And brand new decorating ruined. They had a water-stoppage and the chap 2 floors above me left his tap on... get the picture?! Thank God insurance will cover the cost and, hopefully, not my insurance!!' (Pat Coombs, letter to the author, 5th October 2000)

Index